evo | Octane

THE DREAM 100

evo | Octane

THE DREAM 100

100 YEARS. 100 CARS.
THE GREATEST OF ALL TIME.

Contents

Introduction

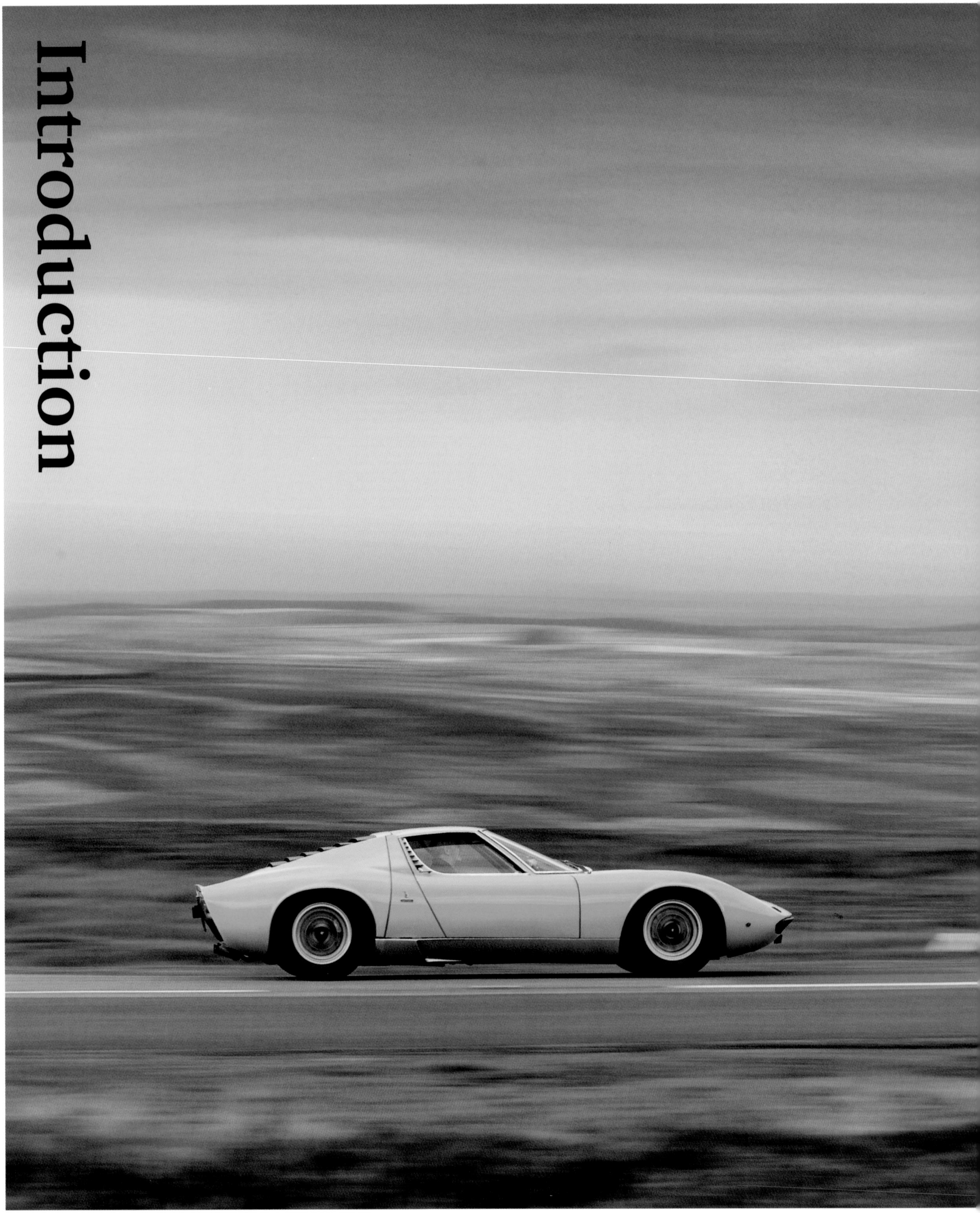

The very best cars inspire fascination, excitement, passion and devotion. It was true 100 years ago and – despite the ever-increasing constraints on their use – it's still true today. Welcome, then, to our rundown of the 100 coolest and most exciting cars of the last 100 years. Enjoy the ride!

T he road testers on *Evo* and *Octane* magazines must be the luckiest in the business. Quite simply, their day job is to drive and assess the world's greatest cars, whether that be a 1920s Bentley or the very latest McLaren supercar. Put it this way: you won't find them behind the wheel of many diesel hatchbacks.

So we asked them a simple question: which cars of the last 100 years excite you the most? Which are the ones that get you fired up and longing to get back behind the wheel? And though there's no denying the thrill of a powerful sports car, it's not just about the fastest, but the most innovative, the most intriguing and the most stylish too.

One thing that all the cars in this book have in common is that they were the standout, landmark machines of their day. So along with the sports cars, you'll find innovative cars that started trends, like the original Mini and the Range Rover, and style icons like the Citroën DS. These are cars that broke the mould and are, to us, every bit as cool as the latest Ferrari.

Our rundown starts just after the First World War, as the motor industry in Europe was slowly getting back on its feet and the wealthy young enthusiasts of the day were eagerly lapping up the first products of the new motoring age. With their spindly wheels and bicycle-style mudguards, their upright radiators and crude controls, the cars of this era look quaint to modern eyes. And yet, if we'd lived in those times, these are the exact cars we'd be enthusing about – comparing power outputs and performance statistics, poring over photographs (black-and -white in those days, of course) in

the motoring press of the day, and hoping to catch a glimpse of them as they rumbled through our towns and villages or kicked up dust on the open road, exhausts blaring.

By the 1930s, cars were no longer the exclusive preserve of the wealthy and yet the decade also saw the rise of fabulously luxurious and powerful machines – the forerunners of today's supercars. And then, after another war, came what many see as a golden age of motoring, a period that ran through the 1950s and '60s and gave us cars like the E-type Jaguar, the Ferrari Berlinettas and, yes, the humble but brilliant Mini.

But there are great cars to be found in every era, whether it's the early supercars of the '70s, the four-wheel-drive rally-bred specials of the '80s and '90s, or the first waves of hypercars and hybrids of more recent times. In these pages we celebrate them all – and put you right there in the driving seat.

Vauxhall *30/98*

In 1920, the car topping the wish list of most rich, young motoring enthusiasts in the UK was a Vauxhall

Unlikely as it may seem, the car on these pages was one of the very first high-performance road cars. Performance is relative, of course, but the 30/98 built by Vauxhall Motors (before it became part of the giant GM group) was the first British car that offered a step-up to a different league, where racing speeds might be achieved on the road, even in standard trim.

Why 30 and why 98? No one knows for sure. It's been suggested that 30bhp is the power output at 1,000rpm, and 98bhp the maximum, but whatever the reason, it's a name that just rolls off the tongue, suggestive of the long, lolloping gait that makes this car such a good all-rounder.

Not that it's an easy drive on first acquaintance. When cold, the gearbox is an unforgiving, recalcitrant thing. But once some heat has soaked through from the big four-cylinder engine, it slides from cog to cog with only an occasional grumble. Double-declutching to help ease the gearshifts through is mandatory and takes a little more time to master.

The footbrake (that's the pedal on the right; the accelerator is placed centrally) works a contracting band on the transmission and its stopping power is, frankly, feeble. The handbrake – that near-vertical lever outside the cabin – is relatively powerful, but it's still a handbrake. It's one of four competing uses for your right arm, which must also change gear, signal a change of direction and help with the steering, which is extremely heavy at low speed.

If you're thinking that the 30/98 sounds like a handful (or several hands-full), you're right. But it's also tremendous fun. The engine is the main reason – such a fruity, sporting noise is accompanied by prodigious grunt and a very un-Edwardian willingness to rev. With only two on board, it romps up hills and makes short work of straights. With factory bodywork like this example, it would do 90mph, but Vauxhall would guarantee 100mph if it was stripped and lightened into racing trim. That means it's a genuine 70mph cruiser today, and one that will run and run.

Production ended in 1927, two years after Vauxhall's takeover by GM. The focus then moved to lower-cost mass production, and the 30/98 was most definitely a car from another age.

SPECIFICATIONS

Years produced: 1919–27 **Engine:** In-line 4-cylinder, 4,224cc **Max power:** 112bhp @ 3,400rpm
Torque: n/a **0–60mph:** n/a **Max speed:** c.90mph
Price: c.£1,000 new in 1919, £500,000+/$640,000+ today

1921

Bentley *3-Litre*

Bentley soon became the marque of choice for gentlemen drivers of a sporting persuasion,
and the 3-Litre was the Bentley they first lusted after

SPECIFICATIONS

Years produced: 1921–29 **Engine:** In-line 4-cylinder, 2,996cc **Max power:** c.90bhp @ 3,500rpm
Torque: n/a **0–60mph:** n/a **Max speed:** 100mph
Price: £895 (plus coachwork) new in 1921, £500,000+/$640,000+ today

It was Le Mans that made Bentley's name. A 3-Litre took part in the very first 24 Hours in 1923, the following year a sister car actually won the race outright, and in 1927 a short-wheelbase 'Super Sports' version – rather like the car here – repeated the feat.

The 3-Litre also made for a charismatic and rapid road car, thanks to its torque-heavy engine. The big four-cylinder was actually very advanced for its time, with four valves per cylinder and dry-sump lubrication, and it made the Super Sports a genuine 100mph car. Driving one today is always an event.

Ingress is through the minuscule nearside door, and the cockpit is very tight. The upright seats are small buckets, and the view over the high scuttle is through a windscreen covered in wire mesh. The large steering wheel is close to your chest, and the black dashboard is full of lovely AT instruments, the red line set at just 3,000rpm on the rev-counter.

Punch the big black starter button. There is a loud clang as the starter engages and the engine fires immediately, then settles down to a slow and low *bub-bub-bub-bub* idle. Now all you have to do is remember that the throttle pedal is in the central position!

The large, drilled gearshift lever is located outboard as the body is so narrow, and it has a very long throw. Lift your foot off the clutch pedal – it has a sharp on/off action – and the Super Sports moves off easily, thanks to the long-stroke engine. The heavy steering lightens instantly and, from the off, the Bentley feels really quite sprightly.

Going for second requires a deliberate pull on the long shifter, a double declutch and the gritting of teeth. You want to get through the whine of third gear and into the quiet of top gear as soon as possible, but it takes practice, with some angry gear-crashing when you get it wrong.

Once it's flowing along, the Bentley is a revelation. The steering is slop-free and alive, the brakes powerful, the ride – despite the short chassis – pliant, and the engine has gobs of mellifluous torque. And soon you know why – in pure driving terms – most enthusiasts agree that of all the classic early Bentleys, the 3-Litre is the one.

1929

Duesenberg *Model J*

The late 1920s saw the rise of a new breed of fabulously powerful and luxurious cars, and the Model J epitomized the breed

D uesenberg's aim was to build a world-class luxury car to challenge the likes of Bugatti or Rolls-Royce. The Model J, launched in 1929, was the result. It was a hugely expensive car – retailing at $8,500 for a rolling chassis and about twice that when custom-bodied – and had a total production run of fewer than 500.

While all Model Js are special, some are more special than most. This one, chassis no J460, dates from 1931 and was bought by wealthy adventurer and playboy George Whittell Jr, who had it custom-bodied by the Walter M Murphy Company of Pasadena, California. Among its special features are lockable compartments behind the front seats – almost certainly specified to conceal bottles of hard liquor, this being the time of Prohibition.

Slide onto the glossy, black patent leather bench seat. The steering wheel is huge, naturally, and the numerous dials seem a long distance away. At first it appears there are two gear levers, but it turns out the second lever opens up the exhaust when a spot of rortiness is called for.

Insert the tiny ignition key, turn it clockwise and pull out the starter knob. The Duesy's huge 6.9-litre straight-eight rumbles into life almost instantly, feeling smooth and insulated from the cabin. Built by Lycoming, it's quite a sophisticated power unit, having double overhead camshafts and four valves per cylinder, but it's tuned for reliability and refinement rather than outright power.

With plenty of torque on tap, the Model J made do with a three-speed gearbox. You need first gear more than you might expect, because second is a tall ratio, good for over 90mph. Maximum speed in top is about 115mph, which means this huge car will sit all day at 70 or 80.

As you'd expect, the steering is massively heavy at parking speeds but beautifully precise and manageable once the car is underway. Goose the throttle and this massive automobile surges forward, its gurgling exhaust note transforming into a spirited thrum – or an attractively masculine rasp, if you've opened the exhaust. The brakes have their work cut out: they are at least servo-assisted but woe betide any modern compact that brakes too sharply in front; the Duesy would simply bulldoze it into a cube of metal like a scrapyard crusher.

SPECIFICATIONS

Years produced: 1929–37 **Engine:** In-line 8-cylinder, 6,883cc **Max power:** 265bhp @ 4,200rpm
Torque: 374lb ft @ 2,000rpm **0–60mph:** n/a **Max speed:** c.115mph
Price: £2m+/$2.6m today

Frazer Nash *Sports*

If you wanted an uncompromising sports car in the 1930s, the chain-driven 'Nash was the car for you

SPECIFICATIONS

Years produced: 1930–39 **Engine:** In-line 6-cylinder, 1,496cc (see text) **Max power:** 75bhp @ 4,800rpm
Torque: n/a **0–60mph:** n/a **Max speed:** c.80mph
Price: £425 new in 1930, £200,000+/$257,000 today

The Frazer Nash was a sports car like no other. The unusual thing about this diminutive Brit was that the rear wheels were driven by a system of chains with no rear differential, which meant both sides of the axle were locked together, which promoted lurid tail-slides, or 'drifts' in modern parlance. Power came from a range of four- and six-cylinder engines, but this particular 'Nash has a later BMW 328 straight-six strapped into the chassis (Frazer Nash was the UK's BMW importer in the 1930s), race-tuned to deliver 145bhp in a car that weighs just 768kg/1,693lb with half a tank of fuel. Of course, big power in a lightweight vehicle is what sports cars are all about. But the 'Nash has the advantage of its chain drive. Most gearboxes lose about 30 per cent of flywheel power, but not so chain drive, which loses a mere 5 per cent.

So you clamber into the tight cockpit and bucket seat, which affords you a great view through the aeroscreen down the long, louvred bonnet. The floor is raw wood, with a foot brace to keep you in the seat during brisk cornering. The large Brooklands sprung wheel is mounted high and various instruments are scattered across the wooden dashboard.

The 2-litre six-cylinder engine with three Solex carburettors responds instantly, with virtually no discernible flywheel effect. The gear lever is outside the cockpit on your right, with the shift pattern the mirror image of what we are used to, so first is further away. Now let the clutch up a tad to allow the gear to mesh with a clunk. Once engaged, the 'Nash leaps off the mark. Second ratio is straight back down, third is towards you and up, fourth straight back. Once you get used to the shifter, the gears swap with alacrity.

Given its head, the 'Nash takes off like a dog with a bone. It is seriously quick, and the speed seems greater because the small screens do little to prevent the wind blast while the whole vehicle fizzes, shakes, rattles and rasps. No wonder enthusiasts love these 'Chain Gang' Frazer Nashes. Vintage, certainly, but with pin-sharp steering, surprisingly effective rod brakes working the large finned front drums, a powerful engine and chuckable chassis, this pure sports car is a revelation – and never mind the chain oil getting everywhere.

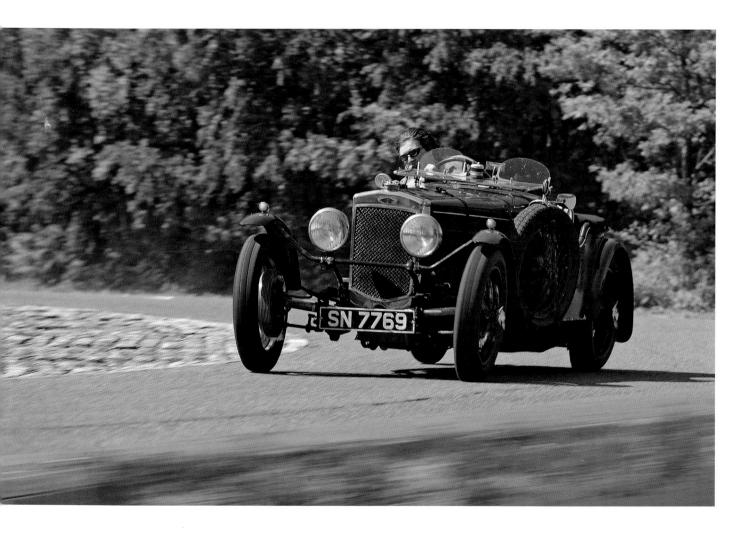

SPECIFICATIONS

Years produced: 1931–39 **Engine:** In-line 8-cylinder, 2,905cc, twin superchargers **Max power:** 180bhp @ 5,200rpm
Torque: n/a **0–60mph:** c.9sec **Max speed:** c.120mph
Price: c.£1,200 (plus coachwork) new in 1931, £20m+/$26m+ today

1931

Alfa Romeo *8C 2900B*

The 8C was the most advanced sports car of the 1930s, and one of the most elegant, too.
For some, this is the first 'supercar'

These 8C 2900s were truly special, and driving them hard was exactly what they were designed for. Of the 40-ish built, many were raced – indeed, 2900s won the Mille Miglia road race a record four times – while long-time Bristol Cars proprietor Tony Crook once famously claimed that his own 2900 had been timed at 132mph.

This particular 2900, chassis 412022 with a body by Touring, is a particularly fine example of the pre-war coachbuilder's art in its original grey with red leather interior – exactly how it looked when it was one of the stars of the 1938 British Motor Show at London's Olympia.

What's under the bonnet is every bit as stunning. The Alfa's engine is genuinely a Grand Prix design, a straight-eight monster with twin superchargers, gear-driven double overhead camshafts and a pair of updraught Weber carburettors. As standard, the power output was around 180bhp, with the capacity for further tuning to take it to 220bhp.

Linked to this was a strong four-speed transaxle, a combined gearbox and differential unit mounted at the rear for the best possible weight distribution; all this in a chassis that was boxed for strength and independently sprung on coils at the front and a transverse leaf spring at the rear, with hydraulic and friction dampers keeping both ends in check. There was no more technically advanced road car of the era than the 8C 2900.

The straight-eight fires instantly and voices have to be raised above the whine of the twin superchargers. The central throttle pedal takes some getting used to, ditto the reverse-H gearshift pattern, with first gear over to the right. Once you've got your head around that, the car is very light and smooth to drive, and the straight-eight revs really well. It's not turbine-smooth like a V12, but it's got a guttural smoothness that's really satisfying. Indeed, the whole car is immensely satisfying to drive. The transaxle is surprisingly easy to shift, and once you're into fourth, the Alfa really settles into a groove. The handling is terrific, the car feeling all of a piece. In fact, its road manners are those of a much younger car.

As you charge off down the road, the exhaust note perfectly defines that old ripping-calico descriptive cliché, battling with the superchargers to make the most noise. The pull is immense, the thrill of speed intoxicating. What a machine!

1936

Jaguar *SS100*

Classic Jaguars always combined dashing good looks, strong performance and great value.
The SS100 was the car that set the template

SPECIFICATIONS

Years produced: 1936–41 **Engine:** In-line 6-cylinder, 2,663cc **Max power:** 105bhp @ 4,500rpm
Torque: 167lb ft @ 2,800rpm **0–60mph:** 12.8sec **Max speed:** 95mph
Price: £395 new in 1936, £350,000+/$275,000+ today

J aguar founder William Lyons wasn't only an astute businessman. He was also a gifted stylist, and the SS100 proves the point. From every angle it looks superb. Some of the 'old school' thought it was a bit caddish at the time, but it was a proper sports car priced at just £395 when new, undercutting everything else on the market. Performance was decent, too, thanks to a new overhead-valve cylinder head for the 2.5-litre straight-six engine (originally a Standard unit), which produced close to 100mph (a larger 3.5-litre engine with a claimed 125bhp arrived in 1938).

Ingress is via a flimsy 'suicide' door into a tight cockpit, and the large Bluemels steering wheel leaves little space for thighs. The seating position is typically arms-out, there is plenty of legroom, although not much space for large feet, and the view along the long, louvred bonnet and widely splayed front wings is terrific.

The engine fires instantly and sounds much larger than its 2½-litre capacity would suggest, sucking through twin 1¼-in SU carbs. The clutch is light, the gear lever requires only a short wrist action into non-synchro first, but the steering is heavy via the flexible rim. Still, the SS100 moves off easily enough.

The gearshift is synchro'd from second but it's best to take it a bit slow. The lovely little straight-six is eager and reacts quickly to accelerator pedal increments, even if the rev band is limited to about 4,500. The steering quickly lightens and the brakes, though not full of feel, certainly work effectively and inspire confidence. Soon you are bowling along at quite a clip, the sensation of speed enhanced by the very open cockpit.

When you start to push the Jaguar, it responds in a benign manner. Going a bit faster into corners, the chassis eases into a drift. You feel the car settle its weight onto the outside tyres, then you unwind a bit of steering lock as the grip gently lets go – all very satisfying and all at legal speeds, though the under-damped rear axle struggles for composure when the road gets rough.

Some regard the SS100 as a bit dandy, but this is dispelled when you drive it. And that's backed up by its competition record, with class and outright wins in international rallying in its day. It's a proper bit of kit.

1936

BMW *328 Roadster*

One of the most advanced of pre-war cars, the pretty 328 was a fine competition device that also made a great road car

Originally known for its aircraft engines, BMW had been producing cars for only five years when it launched the 328 Roadster in 1936, but the new model was a breakthrough in terms of both lightness and speed. It excelled on the European race circuits against the British and Italian competition – and it also made for one of the outstanding road cars of its era.

It certainly looked the part – beautifully engineered and exquisitely proportioned. It was one of the first cars to make extensive use of wind-tunnel testing, while under that shapely body was a stiff, light, tubular frame. Its sophisticated engine produced 80bhp – quite a feat for a 2-litre in 1936, and especially effective in a car weighing only 830kg/1,830lb. Tuned competition versions produced as much as 135bhp.

The example pictured here was supplied new in 1937 to a Polish enthusiast and was raced with considerable success in its early years. It resurfaced in Budapest 25 years ago and has since been restored, complete with a 135bhp Mille Miglia-specification engine. The note of that engine is clear and crisp, the throttle response immediate. The revs climb joyfully and quickly, as in a modern engine, despite the BMW's relatively long 96mm stroke. Indeed, it will rev safely to 6,000rpm. With this much power to pull a modest 830kg, it's not surprising that plentiful performance is achieved with little effort.

There's a good view ahead over a smooth, mascot-free bonnet, and the BMW's narrowness is emphasized by the shapely lines of its front wings. Within just a few miles, the 328 is smooth and easy to handle. Its agility, shock-free steering, light gearchange and good braking make it feel like a much more recent car. Only the suspension sometimes reminds you that it was designed in the mid-1930s.

On a quiet country road, you can start playing with the engine power, delivered with such a spread of torque that you don't need to change gear very often. Long-stroke engines are good for that, providing a wealth of torque that nowadays calls for a turbocharger. And then you approach a curve a little too quickly and discover how easily the BMW's natural oversteer is controlled by the responsive throttle pedal. No wonder that many at the time considered the 328 the best all-round sports car in the world.

SPECIFICATIONS

Years produced: 1936–40 **Engine:** In-line 6-cylinder, 1,971cc **Max power:** 80bhp @ 5,000rpm
Torque: 93lb ft @ 4,000rpm **0–60mph:** c.10sec **Max speed:** 93mph
Price: £695 new in 1936, £500,000+/$640,000+ today

1936

Bugatti *Type 57SC Atlantic*

An automotive sculpture, the Atlantic is as rare and exotic as a car gets –

and today it is one of the world's most coveted machines

SPECIFICATIONS

Years produced: 1936–38 **Engine:** In-line 8-cylinder, 3,257cc, supercharged **Max power:** 210bhp @ 5,500rpm
Torque: n/a **0–60mph:** c.9sec **Max speed:** c.120mph
Price: £40m+/$51m+ today

Bugatti's Type 57SC Atlantic vies with the Alfa 8C 2900 for the title of first ever 'supercar'. In 1937, speed king Sir Malcolm Campbell referred to his own 57SC Corsica roadster as 'the best all-round super-sports car which is available on the market today'. The Atlantic was even more exotic, and its supercharged, double-overhead-cam, straight-eight engine, like its body, was a work of art.

Only four Atlantics emerged from Bugatti's Molsheim factory, and only three survive intact. Today, each is valued at £40m+/$51m+, which is why the car pictured here is actually a replica. Not any old replica, though. Owned by Bugatti itself, it's one of five exact copies built (using genuine Bugatti parts) by Erik Koux. And it's real enough for its sensual mix of beauty and sheer menace to send a tingle down the spine.

Insert yourself through the kidney-shaped door and settle behind the wheel. It's surprisingly light and airy in the cabin, and the view through the windscreen is as evocative as it gets, the wings rising up even higher than the bonnet. Fire the engine and, as with any car of this vintage, there's a background whine of shafts spinning in unsophisticated bearings, accompanied by the trademark whirring of the Type 57's camshaft drive gears, but a blip of throttle results in a gorgeous bark from the exhaust.

The clutch is heavy, but the gear selection is direct and positive. It doesn't need much gas to pull away – you just let the torque do the job – and it doesn't take long to master the precise gearchange, as long as you're willing to feel, rather than crash, the gears home. Double-declutching is a necessity on down changes.

The steering is heavy, to the point that you fear for your ability to heave the wheel effectively enough to make it through tight turns, especially when that deliciously powerful engine has propelled you to speeds that modern arms, pampered by power steering, aren't going to cope with. But, every now and again, it all comes together and starts to flow – the motoring equivalent of the unmistakable 'click' of a perfectly struck golf ball.

What a challenge it would be to drive this wonderful machine on, say, the Mille Miglia Retrospective. The heat would build in the cabin, even with the lever-operated roof vents popped open. The hard suspension would jar every organ. And at the end of the journey your brain would be pulsing with an unmatched sense of achievement and fulfilment.

1948

Porsche *356*

Porsche's first production model was based on the humble VW Beetle but it soon developed

a cult following among keen drivers

SPECIFICATIONS

Years produced: 1948–65 **Engine:** Flat-4-cylinder, 1,582cc **Max power:** 60bhp @ 4,800rpm
Torque: 80lb ft @ 2,800rpm **0–60mph:** 14sec **Max speed:** 100mph
Price: c.£2,000/$3575 new in 1948, £200,000+/$150,000+ today

Ferdinand Porsche's first claim to fame was inventing the VW Beetle, so it was entirely natural that the first Porsche sports cars produced by his son, 'Ferry' Porsche, should be Beetle-based, including the rear-mounted, air-cooled flat-4 engine. From these, on the face of it unpromising, beginnings would grow one of the greatest manufacturers of sporting cars the world would ever know.

After a short run of early examples in Gmünd, Austria, production proper started in Stuttgart in 1950 and would continue right through until 1965, overlapping with the introduction of the more advanced and better-known 911. In that time, the 356 went through more regenerations than Dr Who – the car pictured here is an early 1958 Convertible 'D' with a 60bhp 1.6-litre version of the flat-four (other versions had as much as 95bhp). It's a lot more fun than that lowly power figure might suggest. As enthusiasts in the '50s quickly discovered, it was just the sweetest, lightest, easiest car to drive.

The driver's door pops open and the well-upholstered seat is fat and comfortable. The ivory steering wheel is a masterpiece of design, with a thin, tactile rim, and the six-volt starter just

about cranks the engine into life, the flat-four celebrating with a gruff growl. There's a feather-light clutch and the ivory-topped gearshift wand is delicate, if vague, in action.

On the move, the 'D' seems to swivel from your hips. Its steering, with only 2.26 turns from lock to lock, is delightful. The independent suspension allows you to float across road imperfections at speed, unlike in most 1950s sports cars, yet it is the feeling of robust quality that impresses most. The Drauz-built coachwork (hence the 'D') suffers no noticeable body shake, and the large drum brakes are powerful, engendering a degree of confidence along challenging roads. This is a car that wills you to carry speed in, through and beyond the corners. That's driving satisfaction.

As the owner of this example remarks, it has the most beautiful steering, the engine chugs out enough torque and, being light, it's nippy and agile and feels so beautifully made. Sure, it's not especially fast and it's not the sort of car that you cane the nuts off, but on a twisting mountain road the Porsche 356 is a joy to pedal along swiftly.

1953
Austin-Healey *100*

The 'Big Healey' was the archetypal hairy-chested British sports car,
and the competition-focused 'S' was the hairiest of them all

SPECIFICATIONS

Years produced: 1953–59 **Engine:** In-line 4-cylinder, 2,660cc **Max power:** 132bhp @ 4,750rpm ('S')
Torque: 168lb ft @ 2,500rpm **0–60mph:** 7.8sec **Max speed:** 119mph
Price: special order only when new, £750,000/$965,000 ('S') today

Racer and engineer Donald Healey had been building cars since 1945 but success eluded him until his latest model, the Healey 100, was unveiled at the 1952 British Motor Show at London's Earl's Court and caught the eye of BMC boss Leonard Lord. The manufacturing mogul liked its lines so much that he offered to build it and supply Austin engines, and so the Austin-Healey was born.

The 'big Healey' – so-called to distinguish it from the cheap and cheerful Austin-Healey Sprite that appeared shortly after – later gained a six-cylinder engine and stayed in production as the 3000 until 1962, but the original four-cylinder Healey 100 is the car that first caught the imagination. It was a big hit in the US and spawned several competition versions, of which the alloy-bodied 'S' is the most coveted.

For the 'S', Healey's competitions department took the whacking great long-stroke 2.6-litre 'four' and prodded it from 90 horses up to 132, with a pair of huge 2-in SU carburettors and a steel billet crankshaft that meant it could be properly revved.

It does indeed spin up amazingly for such a big, pushrod four-banger. The side benefit is a throttle response that's really quite impressive, though first gear was clearly intended for full-on competition launches and, combined with the eager throttle, getting away smoothly at a moderate pace does take some practice.

But when you get the hang of it, the 'S' will blast off like a scared rabbit, and a snappy shift to second puts you exactly on the sweet spot of the power band. What's more, second is so tall you can hang on to it seemingly forever. Stay there all through a typical roundabout or, more appropriately, a tight circuit corner before a long straight, and the car will come out pulling like a freight locomotive, with a bellow in your ear from the side-exit exhaust, sending shivers up the spine. The brakes are up to the speed potential, too – hallelujah! – and the suspension has that solid, chuckable feel that Austin-Healeys are famous for: kind of broad-shouldered and ready, and whispering, 'Hey, let's have a go then, right?' It's a wonderful reminder of the time when sports racing cars literally were sports cars you could race.

1954

Mercedes-Benz *300SL*

The 'Gullwing' Mercedes was based on a Le Mans-winning racer and it was just about
the most advanced car on the road in the mid-1950s

SPECIFICATIONS

Years produced: 1954–57 **Engine:** In-line 6-cylinder, 2,996cc **Max power:** 215bhp @ 5,800rpm
Torque: 228lb ft @ 5,000rpm **0–60mph:** c.8sec **Max speed:** 155mph
Price: £4,393/$6,940 new in 1954, c.£1m/$1.3m today

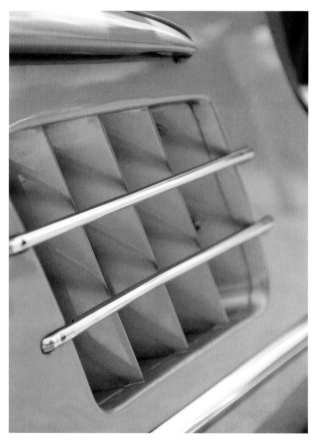

ven today, 155mph is an impressive figure. Well over twice the UK's national speed limit, it also happens to be the speed to which many present-day performance cars are artificially restricted. Imagine, then, how much more outrageous the idea of driving at 155mph must have seemed in the 1950s.

Mercedes' 300SL 'Gullwing', so named for the way its doors opened, was a highly advanced machine with a racing-derived spaceframe chassis, aerodynamic bodywork and a straight-six engine fed by Bosch fuel injection. It was also officially clocked at 155mph.

Lower yourself carefully into the driver's padded bucket seat – the steering wheel can be tilted from the hub, to create much-needed temporary legroom – and you'll notice one of the chassis tubes breaking cover from the deep sill and running into the footwell – a reminder that this is essentially a poshed-up racing car. Pull a knob to enrich the mixture temporarily, turn the key, and the fuel-injected motor starts instantly, sounding smooth and relatively subdued.

Push the tall, spindly gearlever into first and pull away; you're already aware of the Gullwing's heft, something accentuated by the surprisingly long throw when you change up into second. This feels a big car. You can sense the underlying power, sure, but it's a car for the long haul rather than the short sprint.

Wind the engine up through the gears and the smoothness doesn't diminish, although the exhaust note takes on a meaner, harder edge and the car starts to come into its own. That inherent weightiness smooths your path, and the steering is pleasantly damped. The 3-litre engine was designed to run at 6,000rpm almost indefinitely, so you have no qualms about giving it full rein.

In fact, the only qualms are with the 300SL's infamous swing-axle rear suspension. Commit the cardinal sin of lifting off abruptly in a corner, which will cause the high-pivoted swing axles to jack themselves in and play havoc with wheel camber angles, and you'll discover a new meaning of the word 'oversteer'. Drive smoothly, follow the slow-in, fast-out maxim, and the Gullwing will respond obediently.

The great strengths of the 300SL were speed, comfort and utter dependability. You could even listen to American Forces Network on the radio while travelling at three-figure speeds – if you turned the volume up loud.

1955

Citroën *DS*

One of the most remarkable cars ever created, the DS caused a sensation at its launch
and it is still turning heads today

SPECIFICATIONS

Years produced: 1955–74 **Engine:** In-line 4-cylinder, 2,347cc (DS23) **Max power:** 130bhp @ 5,250rpm
Torque: 144lb ft @ 2,500rpm **0–60mph:** 10.4sec **Max speed:** 120mph
Price: £1,977 new in 1955, £30,000+/$39,000+ today

W hen the DS appeared in 1955, it was as though it had landed from another planet. Even its name – in French, DS is pronounced *déesse*, which means goddess – suggested something otherworldly. Its shape, a blend of aerodynamics and a uniquely French style, was just the start. Underneath were sophisticated oleo-pneumatic systems for the suspension, brakes and clutch, with the ride height adjustable from inside the car.

The DS's appearance was further enhanced in 1967 with a new, shark-like nose and glass covers for the headlights, which now swivelled as the steering turned, so that the Goddess could 'see around corners'. The model's one weak spot was also addressed at this time, with a new range of engines replacing the old and rather unrefined 1.9-litre engine that had powered early versions.

But it was in the 1970s in its DS23 form, as pictured here, with a 130bhp 2.3-litre engine, that the DS finally had the performance to match its looks, that slippery body allowing it to reach speeds of up to 120mph. And where better to enjoy it than on a road trip to the wine regions of Europe…?

As you set out, that famous suspension – with conventional springs replaced by cushions of air – is a boon for tackling speed bumps while you relax in the plush brown leather seats. Finished in Rouge Massena, this fuel-injected 1974 DS23 Pallas represents the pinnacle of Flaminio Bertoni's mid-1950s masterpiece. It's loaded with technology: a semi-automatic gearbox, that oleo-pneumatic self-levelling suspension and those swivelling headlights, which made for luxury well ahead of its time. Only the lack of such comparative fripperies as central locking and electric windows betrays its 40-plus years of age.

As a 450-mile drive along the motorways of France, Belgium, Luxembourg and Germany progresses, the car cruises easily at 70mph with modern traffic and delivers mid-30s mpg. The driving position is maybe a little upright but armchair comfort makes a four-hour stint behind the wheel easy.

The abrupt action of the brake pedal takes a little getting used to, and the combination of front-wheel drive and heavily power-assisted steering means the DS is no sports saloon. But once into France, it cruises along smooth, winding roads in serene fashion. And even when loaded with a few cases of wine, it runs level and true thanks to that clever suspension. *Magnifique*!

1957

Jaguar *XKSS*

A barely tamed road-going version of Jaguar's Le Mans-winning D-type, the XKSS was savagely rapid and effortlessly cool

The XKSS is almost too gorgeous, with its wraparound windscreen and pumped-up rear haunches giving it a slightly cartoonish quality. Get closer, though, and that film-star superficiality is displaced by something much more serious. In the engine bay, the exposed chassis tubes, massive oil tank filler cap and oval alloy header tank have the no-compromise feel of a fighter plane, or, indeed, the racing car of which the XKSS is a very lightly disguised version.

The XKSS was a reskinned D-type, made slightly more civilized for the road. This was achieved by deleting the tailfin, adding the wraparound screen and vestigial side screens and bolting on a few fripperies such as bumpers and, most amusingly, a luggage rack. The plan was to make 25 cars but, in February 1957, a major fire ravaged the Browns Lane factory in Coventry after just 16 had been built. As a result, the XKSS is one of the rarest supercars of the 1950s.

If you're tall, it's a squeeze getting your legs around the fixed steering wheel, and you'll have an aching left ankle from keeping the foot lifted away from the clutch pedal. It's all worth it, though, to experience one of the most thrilling and evocative road cars ever made. Thumb the starter button and the XK engine crackles into life with the rich, throaty sound of a big straight-six gulping air through three massive carburettors and blowing it out again from a very un-English side exhaust.

The performance is completely addictive: 250bhp to haul just 920kg/1 ton means that down changes are rarely necessary, although you'll find any excuse to drop a gear and revel in the XK's creamy snarl. The steering is light and sharp, the disc brakes effective – once you give the pedal a good, hard shove. The biggest surprise is the fidgety quality of the ride. A full tank of fuel, all 37 gallons of it, would doubtless make it feel more planted, but this is not a car you can afford to drive on autopilot.

Ah, those aircraft associations again. As the XKSS burbles back to its garage, the note from the side exhaust, reflecting off a tall stone wall, sounds exactly like that of a taxiing Spitfire. That's why the XKSS would be such a fabulous car to live with: it's exciting and demanding enough to make you feel that you've returned safely not just from a drive but from a mission.

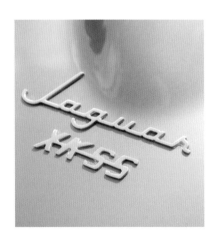

SPECIFICATIONS

Years produced: 1957 **Engine:** In-line 6-cylinder, 3,442cc **Max power:** 250bhp @ 5,750rpm
Torque: 242lb ft @ 4,000rpm **0–60mph:** 5.2sec **Max speed:** 150mph
Price: £2,500/$6,900 new in 1957, £10m+/$12.8m+ today

SPECIFICATIONS

Years produced: 1957– **Engine:** In-line 4-cylinder, 948cc **Max power:** c.50bhp @ 5,000rpm
Torque: n/a **0–60mph:** c.12sec **Max speed:** c.80mph
Price: £611 new in 1957, £20,000+/$35,000+ today

1957

Lotus *Seven*

Built merely as a stopgap, Colin Chapman's lithe little road-racer is still going strong more than 50 years later

Y ou have to wonder what Colin Chapman, founder of Lotus Cars, would have made of the success of the Seven (née Mark VII) today. Conceived one Sunday evening in 1957, it was nothing more than a cheap, light, straightforward competition sports car to replace the successful but, by then, long-in-the-tooth Mark VI. So, after Sunday dinner – to avoid washing the dishes – Chapman and fellow engineer Gilbert 'Mac' McIntosh got their notebooks out. A week later the first car had been built.

The Seven's triumph of longevity stems from the original design: it was just so right. As more power arrived, it was not only the fastest thing on the road but cheap enough for that performance to be accessible – and that remains the case today, with Caterham Cars still building the Seven, having bought the rights way back in 1973.

This early example features a tiny, 948cc, BMC A-series engine. Drop into the seat and cram your legs below the huge steering wheel and you realize that Chapman gave the driver the space needed to work in and no more. The A-series thrums easily into life with a twist of choke, but there's only just enough room to the left of the steering column for your foot to squeeze the direct-action clutch. This makes double-declutch downshifts awkward at first, but means it's all the more satisfying when everything snicks into place.

While not rapid by modern standards, the early Seven is easily quick enough to keep up with traffic and accelerate out of tight spots, the motor revving freely. The steering is light, with a little slack around the straight-ahead – once you've soaked that up, the Seven turns in decisively and with plenty of feel. That encourages you to explore the low grip levels offered by the 4-in tyres. With limited lock, things could get out of hand but, with all information fed back though the steering wheel and lightly padded seat, it's easy to keep things fun rather than unruly. Tiny drum brakes all round would normally be pretty ineffective, but with so little mass they're perfectly adequate.

Today's Caterham Seven is a far quicker machine than the Lotus Seven, but the driving purity and spirit are as strong now as they ever were, and a drive in either is enough to understand just why the car has been popular for so long.

1957

Ferrari *250 California Spyder*

Immortalized in a 1980s cult movie, the California Spyder is quite simply

the most desirable classic road-going Ferrari ever

SPECIFICATIONS

Years produced: 1957–61 **Engine:** V12, 2,953cc **Max power:** 240bhp @ 7,000rpm (SWB)
Torque: 198lb ft @ 5,500rpm **0–60mph:** c.6sec **Max speed:** c.135mph
Price: $14,000 new in the US in 1957, £10m+/$12.8m today

As most Ferrari fans know, the car actually used in *Ferris Bueller's Day Off* was a glass-fibre replica. Even in the mid-1980s, a California Spyder was far too valuable to use in a low-budget flick. Today, a real one could be worth just about anything upwards of £10m/$12.8m. This 1961 car is a short-wheelbase model – with just 55 built, it is the most coveted variant of all, with the classic 3-litre Ferrari V12 engine (shared with the 250 GT SWB and the immortal 250 GTO racer) and sublime Pininfarina bodywork.

Chances to drive one today are fleetingly rare, but even on the night-time streets of London, the Cali Spyder's star quality shines through. There's something very special about piloting an open car through the city at night, and it doesn't matter whether you're in a Ferrari or a Fiat, your senses come alive in a uniquely invigorating way.

Like all classics, the California seems compact and almost dainty compared with almost every other vehicle that surrounds it. From the driver's seat, you feel you could stretch out and touch each extremity with your fingertips, and that gives confidence in traffic. It fires up instantly, as it has done throughout the photography session, and within seconds of leaving our photo location on the banks of the Thames, we're mixing with the black cabs and double-decker buses on Putney Bridge.

The car is lively and agile, darting in and out of gaps in the traffic like a minnow between trout, while you try not to remember that this car has no bumpers or overriders to protect its voluptuous curves. That vulnerability aside, the Spyder makes the perfect city car. It steers nicely, with enough feel and feedback to be comfortable without being nervous, and the four-speed gearshift is positive and satisfyingly mechanical in action. There are four-wheel disc brakes, so no worries on that score, and because you're rolling in a mobile bathtub, you're treated to the full surround sound of that Ferrari V12, its crisp blare bouncing back from shop windows and underpass walls.

The fact is, whether you live in London, LA or Little Plumpton (it's in Lancashire), the California Spyder will never disappoint. As Ferris Bueller put it in 1986, with all the accumulated wisdom only a teenager can possess: 'It is so choice. If you have the means, I highly recommend picking one up.' He's not wrong.

1959

Ferrari *250 GT SWB*

The Ferrari aficionado's favourite Ferrari, the 250 GT Short Wheelbase was equally at home on the road as on the racetrack

T he allure of the 250 GT SWB starts with its perfect Pininfarina proportions – a mixture of beauty and tension that's rarely been bettered. The reduction in wheelbase made the model lighter and easier to hustle through the bends than earlier 250 GTs – it was just that little bit more alive and responsive.

Its handling was also helped by the fitment of telescopic dampers and disc brakes – both Ferrari road-car firsts. And then there was that wonderful, high-revving V12 engine. The road car had a quoted output of 240bhp. In race tune, with around 280bhp – like the car here – it was a genuine 160mph machine, as measured on the Mulsanne Straight at Le Mans. Competition cars had lighter alloy bodies too.

The 250 GTO that followed is the more feted Ferrari in the wider world and was even more successful in competition – that's reflected in the fact that examples now change hands for £40m-plus – but the GTO was a purer racer and is marginal as a road car. The SWB is a true dual-purpose machine, which in road trim makes a very decent fist of its GT role, while on the circuits, in the hands of drivers like Stirling Moss, it was the car to beat. In either role, its beautifully balanced handling was the key, but there's no denying the aural magic of the V12.

Driving this car on the canyon roads of northwest LA, where the tarmac is smooth and grippy, the locals tolerant and the views spectacular, a riptide of aural violence blasts out of the Ferrari's quadruple tailpipes. This bounces off the rock faces to clash with the cacophony of V12 mechanical madness, a whirr of thrashing valve train and dinky-sized pistons flying up and down at 5,000, 6,000, even 7,000rpm.

You can't resist dropping the door windows to take in the noise as you grin like a kid at every blip of the throttle. Foot down and the triple Webers suck so hard it's a wonder that the super-light aluminium bonnet doesn't turn concave, the intake bellow briefly drowning out both engine and exhaust before they fight back with a scream and a roar. And so we continue on our noisily rapid way, sometimes pushed hard into the bucket seats by the acceleration and occasionally backing off to take in the view. What a machine!

SPECIFICATIONS

Years produced: 1959–62 **Engine:** V12, 2,953cc **Max power:** 280bhp @ 7,000rpm
Torque: 203lb ft @ 5,500rpm **0–60mph:** c.6sec **Max speed:** c.160mph
Price: £6,326/$12,600 new in 1959, £7.5m+/$9.6m today

1960

Aston Martin *DB4 GT Zagato*

When David Brown bought Aston Martin, the British marque began its golden age,
and the absolute pinnacle was the DB4 GT Zagato

T he most coveted of all Aston Martin road cars is also one of the most beautiful cars ever built. Not the least remarkable thing about it is that its designer, Ercole Spada, was just 23 and had only just joined styling house Zagato. The Aston was his very first design. Equally remarkable is that Aston struggled to sell them and called a halt after just 20 cars had been built, of which 19 survive. Today, any one of those cars is worth in excess of £10m/$12.8m.

Based on the DB4 GT, which was a lighter and more powerful version of the 'regular' DB4, the Zagato was yet lighter and more powerful – more aerodynamic, too, making it a genuine 150mph-plus car. Some were racers, but most were

road cars – including the superb original example here, chassis number 0178, still wearing its original red paint.

Being careful not to lean on any of the extremely light aluminium body panels, you open the flyweight alloy door with its Perspex window and savour the aroma of gently worn Connolly leather. The open-back chairs with their seat buttons look small but, once you're in position, prove comfortable, if short in the back and not as luxurious as the full DB4 jobs.

Turn the ignition key, give the three Weber carbs a few priming pumps and the six spins on the starter then fires with a big sound. A bit more throttle clears the choke tubes and the engine settles down to idle. It sounds as big and as heavy as it

SPECIFICATIONS

Years produced: 1960–63 **Engine:** In-line 6-cylinder, 3,670cc **Max power:** 314bhp @ 6,000rpm
Torque: 278lb ft @ 5,400rpm **0–60mph:** 6.1sec **Max speed:** 154mph
Price: £5,470 new in 1960, £10m+/$12.8m today

looks under the bonnet but it is refined and not excessively noisy.

The clutch pedal is not particularly heavy but it has a long movement. Select first with the little gearshifter and you find that the Aston needs some revs when moving off due its high first gear. The Webers snuffle and pop a bit but, once sucking air, smooth out and deliver the power. The gearshift is smooth and slick, and the gear ratios are tightly stacked. Squeeze the throttle pedal and the Aston attacks tight mountain bends with enthusiasm. The rack-and-pinion steering is sharp and the Zagato feels significantly livelier and more responsive than the standard DB4.

As you start to give the Aston its head through some of the faster sections, you notice how soft and pliant the ride is. Unfortunately, the rear shocks are imprecise Armstrong lever-arm dampers that – combined with the Aston's weight and less-than-rigid chassis – allow the Zagato to wallow more than you might like. Ferrari's rival SWB feels more precise and wieldy than the Aston and is therefore faster though the bends.

But the Zagato's engine, especially its fat gob of torque that comes into play smack in the middle of the rev-range, more than makes up for its rather vintage handling. The exhaust note is as classy as you get, the big engine willing you to cream it up to the red line where it reacts with sonorous enthusiasm. On faster B-roads, the Aston really comes into its own. With the view along the evocative double-bubble bonnet, enhanced by the sight of a fat rear haunch in the rearview mirror, the Zag bowls along, guided gently via that superb thin-rimmed steering wheel. It is a proper thoroughbred that makes its driver feel like a million dollars. Actually, more like ten million dollars.

1961

Mini-*Cooper*

The forerunner of every hot hatch, on a mission to bring power to the people,
was the effervescent Mini-Cooper

SPECIFICATIONS

Years produced: 1961–71 **Engine:** In-line 4-cylinder, 1,275cc (1275 S) **Max power:** 76bhp @ 5800rpm
Torque: 80lb ft @ 3,000rpm **0–60mph:** 10.5sec **Max speed:** 98mph
Price: £756/$1,495 new in 1961, £30,000+/$21,000+ today

A lec Issigonis's 1959 Mini was a truly remarkable device, but it had been conceived as an economy car, not a performance car. Fortunately for generations of enthusiasts, Issigonis knew Formula One constructor John Cooper from pre-war days when they both raced specials and invited him to drive a prototype. Cooper immediately spotted the Mini's potential with its wonderfully direct steering and tenacious front-wheel-drive handling. Give it some more power and better brakes and it would be a winner on the track and in rallies, he reckoned.

He was right. With an uprated engine, improved gearchange and disc brakes, the Mini-Cooper was an instant hit when it went on sale in 1961. But it was the souped-up Mini-Cooper S, released in 1963, that really created the Mini legend, winning the Monte-Carlo Rally three times. And as a road car, it was an absolute blast. The 1275cc Cooper S was the ultimate: with 76bhp on tap, it was very nearly a 100mph machine out of the box.

A chance to drive a racing version is, of course, too good to pass up. The car here raced extensively in the period and makes about 100bhp. Even if you've driven plenty of hot Minis, this is a whole new feeling. It's not so much that it's fast (although 6,300rpm is easily reached on a long straight in top), it's the almost bonkers degree of friskiness that's surprising – the engine is very 'torquey'.

In the corners, you can feel that mobile rear end and know the front wheels can pull a slide straight in a nanosecond as well as turning in ultra-quickly, loading the tail as they do so.

Best to steel yourself to keep the power flowing, but then you wonder if it will understeer too much, and then spin if you back off… It feels like you're on a knife-edge, but you aren't. It just appears that way because the car seems to pivot around a point just behind the driver according to the position of your right foot.

Soon you're getting the hang of it and starting to trust this tiny car. All the while, the steering is vibrating, the accelerator pedal is too high and you keep sliding out of the seat on the two left-handers, so you're leaning on that lightweight door. It doesn't matter; this is brilliant fun, and you don't want it to end.

SPECIFICATIONS

Years produced: 1961–75 **Engine:** In-line 6-cylinder, 4,235cc (4.2) **Max power:** 265bhp @ 5,500rpm
Torque: 280lb ft @ 4,000rpm **0–60mph:** 7.4sec **Max speed:** 145mph
Price: £1,896/$5,895 (4.2 S1) new in 1961, £120,000+/$154,000+ today

1961

Jaguar *E-Type*

With the looks, performance, handling, refinement – and a bargain price – the E-type had it all

T he E-type was a sports car from the future. In 1961, normal cars could manage about 80mph, with most sports cars reaching 100mph – just. The E-type famously clocked 150mph. And, yes, that test car had been carefully 'prepared' by the factory, but the point was still made. What's more, not only was the new Jaguar traffic-stoppingly beautiful, it was also about a third of the price of anything remotely comparable from Aston Martin or Ferrari.

The Jaguar E-type was derived from the Le Mans-winning D-type, which boasted an advanced monocoque tub and spaceframe construction. The E-type's fully independent rear suspension brought an extra level of sophistication compared with the D-type's solid rear axle, while under the bonnet was the tried-and-tested XK engine in triple-carburettor, 265bhp guise.

In fact, the early 3.8-litre cars had cooling and electrical gremlins, but these were sorted for the 4.2-litre model, launched in October 1964. The larger capacity engine had extra torque and was mated to an improved, four-speed, all-synchromesh gearbox. For most people, this car is the pick of the E-type timeline.

The driver's door is small and you have to wriggle into the cockpit, but what a joy once you're ensconced. The dash is fabulous, with big Smiths instruments and rows of switches. You sit low, in a very comfortable leather seat, the bonnet stretching way out in front, and the big 4.2-litre engine starts quietly on the button, the SU carbs affording a gentle idle. The gearshift is the usual H-pattern and the Jaguar eases off as you'd expect with 280lb ft of torque from the long-stroke six.

All the controls are weighty, especially the rack-and-pinion steering, though that's partly down to slightly wider modern rubber on this car. The suspension is properly set up, so it corners with accuracy and assurance.

At first it's quiet and refined, the engine almost muted. But when the roads open up, the big six takes a breath and the Jaguar lunges. In standard spec, an E-type will dash to 60mph in around seven seconds and 100mph in 16 seconds. This example feels every bit that fast – and sounds glorious.

It's a beguiling car, the E-type. It remains quiet and civilized when pottering, but snarls and takes off when you depress the throttle, and it feels wonderfully planted at speed. It's still casting its spell.

1962

AC *Cobra*

There are few cars as recognizable as an AC Cobra – and driving one quickly is every bit as hairy as its looks would suggest

It was racer Carroll Shelby's idea to fit big Ford V8s into the pretty, English-built AC Ace. The result was designed primarily for racing, but in the process Shelby created one of the most animalistic road cars ever built.

Early examples had 4.2- and 4.7-litre engines, but for the 1965 season it was decided more power was needed and the 'big-block' 427ci V8 (a mighty 7 litres) was the favoured choice. A rapid development programme – assisted by Ford – ensued. To enable the 'side-oiler' engine to fit, the car was widened and its wheel arches were flared provocatively to accommodate the new Halibrand magnesium alloy wheels. Cooling intakes were enlarged, the transmission tunnel widened and the engine moved back in the chassis to maintain weight distribution. In the end, every component was upgraded, although it wasn't enough to tame the 425bhp's hold over the chassis… The sheer scale of the 427's performance would become apparent when Chris Amon tested the factory prototype in October 1964. The 427 demolished 0–100mph in 8.8 seconds.

Having been designed for competition, the 427 was never homologated, as AC hadn't built the requisite 100 cars in time, and in the end many were sold as S/C (semi-competition) road cars. This is one such car in the pictures.

There's no mistaking the seriousness of the NASCAR-derived V8 when it erupts in noise at start-up. Inhaling through a big Holley four-barrel carburettor and exhaling through unmuffled sidepipes, the pushrod V8 makes the whole car jump and shudder like an imbalanced washing machine on 'spin'. And that's just at idle.

On the move, the Cobra snorts and bellows – and demands your full attention as you come to terms with the character and magnitude of the control responses. Slow, unassisted manual steering with a dead spot on-centre increases the arm flailing required during swift cornering. Likewise, the high-effort braking is off the chart for drivers reared on modern cars. And the abundant torque makes the Cobra's line through turns as dependent on throttle position as it is on the angle of the steering wheel. So it's challenging to drive, but the rewards are huge. Slewing half-sideways through racetrack curves, sawing at the steering wheel while the sidepipes bellow, is an experience intense enough to make the hairs on the back of your neck stand on end. For weeks afterward.

SPECIFICATIONS

Years produced: 1962– **Engine:** V8, 6,998cc (427 MkIII) **Max power:** 425bhp @ 6,000rpm
Torque: 480lb ft @ 3,700rpm **0–60mph:** 4.2sec **Max speed:** 165mph
Price: $5,995 new in the US in 1962, £750,000+/$1m+ today

Lotus *Elan*

Anything designed by Colin Chapman was touched with genius, and the Elan would prove
one of the most nimble, tactile and lovable sports cars ever made

SPECIFICATIONS

Years produced: 1962–73 **Engine:** In-line 4-cylinder, 1,558cc **Max power:** 115bhp @ 6,000rpm
Torque: 108lb ft @ 4,000rpm **0–60mph:** 7.6sec **Max speed:** 122mph
Price: £1,499/$4,195 new in 1962, £50,000/$33,000 today

y the early 1960s, Colin Chapman was moving Lotus's road cars away from their kit-car roots. He'd started the process with the Elite of 1958, but the car that established Lotus as a real force in the mainstream was the Elan. With mostly Ford mechanicals but a backbone chassis and suspension of Chapman's own design, all clad in lightweight glass fibre, the benchmarks it set for handling would last for decades.

Elans attracted a mechanically minded, thrill-seeking sort of owner, but not even their greatest fans would cite robustness and durability among the tiny car's many virtues. They are fragile, demanding cars to own, although their gossamer weight, punchy power and telepathic controls make them hugely satisfying, along with a crisp, punchy engine, steering of total transparency, and a benign, confident handling balance. Best of all was the Sprint, which was genuinely rapid, but all of them were hugely engaging, like this early 1968 S4 DHC.

It looks tiny and anyone over six feet might wonder if they'll even fit inside, but there's actually plenty of room, partly because the seat is set low within the chassis. Turn the key in the middle of the slightly incongruously wood-veneered dashboard and the 1.6-litre twin-cam engine tickles into life. The gearbox is really positive to engage and you can immediately sense how little weight there is as you move off.

You expect sweet but obviously classic, low-grip handling, with the steering being the highlight and making up for any lack of pace in the corners. You expect it to be mostly about atmosphere and character. How wrong can you be? It may be more than half a century old, it may have Triumph Herald front suspension, a Ford Cortina engine and gearbox, and a Ford Anglia rear diff, but it's a car that simply doesn't seem to know its age. Turn-in is quick, the chassis summons surprising levels of grip from tiny tyres, the brakes are great. And then there's the engine, which is just so damn eager. It revs so enthusiastically round to 6,000rpm and beyond that you find yourself in fourth, thinking it really could handle another ratio.

So you find yourself overtaking modern cars. The Elan is so small that you can jink comfortably through gaps, and the steering so precise that you never waver. The genius of Colin Chapman should never be underestimated.

1962
Alpine *A110*

The current A110 may be a definite future classic, but this was the jewel-like original

SPECIFICATIONS

Years produced: 1962–77 **Engine:** In-line 4-cylinder, 1,565cc **Max power:** 125bhp @ 6,250rpm
Torque: 117lb ft @ 5,450rpm **0–60mph:** 7.1sec **Max speed:** 130mph
Price: £100,000/$130,000 today

R acing driver Jean Rédélé was the brains behind Dieppe-based Alpine, which started building Renault-based coupés in the 1950s. Its breakthrough came with the 1962 A110, which went on to international fame as a multiple rally winner – and also happened to be one of the coolest-looking cars on the planet.

Like all Alpines, the A110 had a steel backbone chassis, lightweight glass-fibre bodywork and any one of a number of Renault engines mounted in the tail, driving the rear wheels. The 1.6 in this late example is a bit tweaked over standard, with 140-or-so bhp, thanks to a hot camshaft, and a pair of Weber 45 DCOEs – as you fire up, the megaphone tailpipe on the end of the minimal silencer makes sure everyone knows that fact.

This is a very compact car, low with a narrow cockpit, and it's very snug inside, your left shoulder touching the lightweight door, arms angled towards the car's centre, with the legs even more so and almost horizontal, as in a racing car.

Foot down, the tail squats, the already light steering goes even lighter. On a damp road the Alpine's natural thrust is a degree or two either side of straight-ahead, so keeping it absolutely true requires concentration. And it's certainly quick, as you'd expect when this eager motor has just 700kg/1,543lb to push. Below 3,400rpm it's a bit flat and surge-prone but it blares along happily enough. Above that speed the Webers cackle and blatter, the exhaust trumpets and every bit of throttle travel adds another spurt of energy. And because you're sitting so low, the road seems to rush past at a frantic rate, making 70mph feel like 100.

Being a late example, this one has wishbone rear suspension; earlier cars had swing axles, which could give tricky handling. On a near-deserted road with a strong sense of the forest stage about it, the A110 snorts through the curves, the steering garrulous, and the tail mostly planted on the damp surface except when you dither over a bend's apex and back off, provoking an admonitory twitch aft.

This is one talkative car. You sense how the tail calls the shots, how the throttle is as much of a guidance system as the steering wheel, how the expected initial understeer never really happens. And because you always know what's happening, the Alpine is never scary. No wonder the rally drivers loved it.

1963

Chevrolet *Corvette*

Chevrolet is one of the great American marques, the Corvette its legendary sports car,

and the Sting Ray 427 the fiercest of the breed

SPECIFICATIONS

Years produced: 1963–67 (Sting Ray C2) **Engine:** V8, 6,997cc (427) **Max power:** 435bhp @ 5,600rpm
Torque: 460lb ft @ 4,000rpm **0–60mph:** 5.5sec **Max speed:** 145mph
Price: $4,084/$4,037 new in 1963, £150,000/$56,000+ today

Conceived as an image-builder for the Chevrolet brand, the Corvette first appeared way back in 1953. But it was with the C2 generation that it really hit the big time. And the Sting Ray 427 was the full-fat, big-block mother of all 'Vettes. Those 427 cubic inches convert to almost 7 litres. Oh, and 435bhp and 460lb ft of torque. Road testers found it would hit 60mph in 5.5 seconds and max out at 145mph. But that doesn't tell you the half of it.

You expect it to spin its Goodyear tyres off the line, and you expect more tyre-smoke when you select second – maybe a fulsome chirrup as third slots home, too. When you get the same chirrup as you select top gear, you start to pay attention. What you don't expect is the fearsome sensation as you push the long throttle pedal to the stop in top gear when you're already past 100mph. That's when the real power kicks in. The engine note changes, the big-block V8 takes a deep inhalation of juice through its sextet of carburettor throats and, incredibly, erupts. The car squats and the rear tyres spin, again. And that's when you'd really better have your wits about you.

Who needs corners, who need handling, balance, poise and chassis control? This is an adrenalin rush of the first order!

Driving the Sting Ray fast is, of course, an exhilarating experience. But what is it like driving slowly on real roads? Friendly, benign even. Drop into the driver's seat and you can't fail to notice that the trim and fittings are rather cheap-looking. You are met with a thin-rimmed steering wheel, which is no bother because it's power-assisted. Start the engine and the noise erupts from just below the driver's door. With twin sidepipes, you initially think the engine is misfiring but then realize you are only able to hear one bank. Depress the clutch: Toyota soft. Unbelievable. And the 'Vette just trundles off at the lift of the pedal. No need to bother the accelerator.

The gearshift action is lovely and precise and none too heavy. The triple, twin choke Holley carbs can fuel up after a lot of dawdling and need an occasional blast to clear, but that's it. In normal driving, the Corvette is a pussycat. And that's perhaps the greatest surprise of all.

1963
Lotus-*Cortina*

These days, family cars are often given a sporting twist; in 1963, the Lotus Cortina caused a minor sensation

SPECIFICATIONS

Years produced: 1963–66 **Engine:** In-line 4-cylinder, 1,558cc **Max power:** 115bhp @ 6,000rpm
Torque: 108lb ft @ 4,500rpm **0–60mph:** 13.8sec **Max speed:** 108mph
Price: £1,100 new in 1963, £40,000+/$52,000+ (racers £80,000+/$104,000+) today

In the early 1960s, Ford hatched a plan to go saloon car racing with its new saloon and turned to Lotus for technical help. Lotus boss Colin Chapman welcomed the timely injection of funds and commissioned a twin-cam head for the Ford 'Kent' engine. With capacity upped to 1,558cc, this soon-to-be classic unit was inserted into the Cortina hull, along with reworked suspension and light alloy skins for the doors, bonnet and boot lid. And so was born one of the must-have cars of the 1960s.

The original plan called for 1,000 units to be homologated, but it was such a hit with road drivers as well as racers that more than three times that number were built. On the road they were great fun; on the track they were spectacularly quick, especially in the hands of Jim Clark. An ex-Clark car is shown here, and a chance to drive it is not to be missed.

With a squat ride height, side-exiting exhaust and steel rims, 166RUR looks purposeful and period cool. This is how Lotus-Cortinas should be, all pared-back with no flashy addenda. Inside, the cabin is as functional as functional gets.

Lotus-Cortinas always were on the basic side and you wouldn't want it any other way.

With a Vegantune-hotted-up four, it's noisy as hell on start-up: raucous and angry with a slightly metallic timbre. Thanks to a low first gear, initial acceleration past 4,000rpm is eager, although it pulls less strongly from second to third. The actual lever movement is vague, as is to be expected of a Lotus-Cortina, and it's all too easy to grandma a shift when trying to race your changes. You get used to it apparently. Pile on the revs, and it's fast. Not peaky fast like your modern twin-cams but keep it within its natural rev range (it's happiest at 4,000–5,500rpm) and it romps along, cannoning sound out the sidepipe like buckshot.

The steering requires constant corrections, but few cars communicate quite like this. You're aware of every nuisance of road surface, each dimple in the asphalt, and you adjust to suit. In corners it takes on a delightfully neutral to slight oversteer cornering stance with a bit of a hop and a skip should there be bumps. This is such an involving car. Any Lotus-Cortina is cool, but this one tops the lot.

1964

Porsche *911*

Hard to believe now, but when it first appeared, enthusiasts weren't sure about the new Porsche – until they drove it

Back in 1963 when the new Porsche was revealed at the Frankfurt Motor Show, it was not universally liked: here was a bigger, plainer and more expensive car to replace the beloved, curvaceous 356 that had developed such a loyal following. But good engineering will win out, and the 911 offered lightweight construction, more space and refinement, and better handling with rack-and-pinion steering and revamped suspension. Oh, and a brand-new 2-litre, 130bhp flat-six. The 1967 911S was a sweet spot for early 911s, with an increase in power to 160bhp on Weber carburettors, forged alloy Fuchs wheels, anti-roll bars front and rear, and vented disc brakes all round. Today it looks small, even dainty, but the interior is surprisingly roomy and visibility is excellent.

Depress the throttle to halfway to open the six butterflies in the Weber carbs, allow a bit of a churn and the flat-six catches with a *wang*. The response to the light throttle pedal is immediate. It is alive just sitting still: already you can feel the tingle of the vocal and boisterous engine through your bum and fingertips, connecting you directly to the car.

The offset clutch pedal is laughably light, and while the gear lever has a long throw, it's beautifully smooth in action. Plenty of revs and it slings away, the benefit of low kerbweight. Performance is strong even by today's standards. From a standstill it will crack 60mph in seven seconds and top out at 138mph – which is plenty.

Up through the tightly stacked gear ratios, once past 3,500rpm the engine lunges toward the red line, getting smoother all the way, revving happily to 7,000rpm. The steering is fingertip-light and reactive. The Porsche darts along country lanes with vim, the ventilated disc brakes giving reassuring bite.

The ride is supple, soft even. The skinny Michelin XAS radials impart the feeling of dancing, the car on its toes. It is so responsive. Turn-in is immediate, though push a bit harder and the Porsche begins to understeer – but not by much. On these roads there is no indication of oversteer, but then that happens only if you lift off mid-corner at high speed.

This 911 is very intelligently engineered, but it is still sufficiently quirky to reward good driving, and challenging enough to amuse you every time you climb inside. And that, in a nutshell, is why it's lasted 56 years and counting.

SPECIFICATIONS

Years produced: 1964– **Engine:** Flat 6-cylinder, 1,991cc (911S) **Max power:** 160bhp @ 6,600rpm
Torque: 132lb ft @ 5,200rpm **0–60mph:** 7sec **Max speed:** 138mph
Price: £3,556/$6,370 (911S) new in 1964, £150,000+/$140,000+

1964

Ford *Mustang*

The Mustang was Ford's sport car for the masses – and they quickly took it to their hearts

SPECIFICATIONS

Years produced: 1964–68 **Engine:** V8, 4,727cc (289 Fastback) **Max power:** 200bhp @ 4,400rpm
Torque: 282lb ft @ 2,400rpm **0–60mph:** 9.1sec **Max speed:** 116mph
Price: £1,925/$2398 new in 1964, £30,000/$25,000 today

N ot every Mustang has eight cylinders under its long, flat bonnet. Entry-level early ones had a straight-six, later ones had V6s, while the energy-crisis micro-Mustangs of the early 1970s – the ones most car fans try to forget – used a Ford Pinto-donated four-pot. Until the current car, one thing they did all have in common was a solid, live rear axle – with all the limitations that brings in ride comfort and adhesion on imperfect road surfaces. The mix of this axle and the ample thrust of a good V8 ensured both an engagingly retro feel to the driving dynamics and ruined the Mustang's chances of competing with sophisticated Europeans.

None of this mattered to the legions of US buyers who flocked to the Mustang in the mid-1960s, embracing Ford's sports car for the masses. In less than two years, a million had been sold. And the Mustangs that captured their imagination had – of course – a big V8 under the bonnet, as is the case with the 289 (that's 4.7 litres) Fastback in the pictures here.

Inside, thin pillars frame an upright windshield and the steering wheel has a thin, large-diameter rim in wood, part of the much-prized 'Pony' interior, which also includes a five-

dial instrument pack. Under the bonnet is a gentle version of Ford's 289 V8, with a relaxed 200bhp, driving the rear wheels through a three-speed Cruise-O-Matic autobox. It feels brisk enough but, ideally, you'd want the 271bhp Hi-Po option and a four-on-the-floor gearbox.

Its age shows up the most when you turn the steering wheel. Today's chassis engineers are hell-bent on minimizing body roll, but a little lean never did anyone any harm, provided the build-up is nice and progressive. Only once the body has settled and the sinews tautened does the Mustang actually change direction, which it does with a pleasing verve as it loads up the outer rear wheel. So you take a series of bends in a series of broad arm-sweeps and throttle-squeezes. Very old-school.

The fun is that you're fully involved in the driving process. And then there's all the joy of the history, the loyalty that old Mustangs generate and that Ford threw away when the breed turned lardy in the early 1970s. Lee Iacocca, the Ford marketing genius whose idea the Mustang originally was, famously said of these unloved later cars: 'The Mustang market never left us. We left it.'

1965
Alfa *Giulia Sprint GTA*

Developed to win on track, the GTA version of Alfa's delectable Giulia Sprint also made a cracking road car

SPECIFICATIONS

Years produced: 1965–69 **Engine:** In-line 4-cylinder, 1,570cc **Max power:** 115bhp @ 6,500rpm
Torque: 110lb ft @ 4,000rpm **0–60mph:** 8.5sec **Max speed:** 115mph
Price: £2,128 new in 1965, £250,000/$320,000 today

I f it looks right, it probably is right, so they say. The standard 'step front' Alfa Giulia Sprint GT, penned by the young maestro Giorgetto Giugiaro at Bertone, always looked right. Square-edged enough not to render it too dainty, the deliciously compact coupé was beautifully balanced and totally fit for purpose. And the GTA – A for *alleggerita*, or 'lightened' – was all of that and more.

Or rather less, for its development involved obsessive attention to paring away unnecessary weight, starting with reskinning the car in lightweight alloy bodywork, while the tough and reliable twin-cam engine was enlivened with a twin-plug head. Inside there was minimal sound deadening, little bucket seats, and a lovely drilled wood-rim steering wheel. In total, around 200kg/440lb was shed for a dry weight of just 820kg/1,808lb, and the GTA's effectiveness was proved when it became the first Touring Car to lap the infamous Nürburgring Nordschleife in under ten minutes.

Homologation meant building road cars, too, and the GTA Stradale (Italian for 'street') was an absolute corker. In recent times, it's become highly sought-after, and some companies now offer uprated cars with considerably more

power than the original's 115bhp – such as the Alfaholics GTA-R in the photos, which has a storming 222bhp. But an original GTA is still an absolute joy, from the moment you approach it.

The delicate door catch calls to mind a Ferrari Dino's as the light door swings open. The bucket seat is low and snug. The engine fires and emits that lovely Weber gurgle, but the Alfa needs revs to pull away, as the carbs are not happy below 3,000rpm. Beyond that point, however, the engine really wants to rev and just gets smoother towards the top end while emitting a hard, staccato rasp.

Visibility is excellent as the 'box snicks up through the tightly stacked ratios into fifth gear. Meanwhile, the suspension is pliant but controlled, and the GTA feels light and nimble but not nervous. As the lanes open up, the Alfa comes alive, the worm-and-roller steering proving light and accurate. It leans quite a lot into corners, but once you've chosen your line, the GTA just stays on it, the handling essentially benign and flattering, allowing you to work both ends up to and then over their limits. The Alfa GTA looks fabulous, but it is even better to drive.

Lamborghini *Miura*

The first mid-engined supercar was also, in many people's eyes, the most beautiful,

and the Miura's magic remains undimmed

SPECIFICATIONS

Years produced: 1966–71 **Engine:** V12, 3,929cc **Max power:** 370bhp @ 7,700rpm (S)
Torque: 286lb ft @ 5,500rpm **0–60mph:** 6sec **Max speed:** 170mph
Price: £10,860/$20,000 new in 1966, £1.3m/$1.7m today

O ther, much earlier cars can be considered supercars of their time, but the Miura is the one that set the template for what most people now regard as a supercar: a fantastically powerful engine, usually a V12 and placed behind the driver; low, wide and wondrously exotic bodywork; a leather-lined cabin and an impossibly laid-back driving position, the whole concoction fabulously rare and expensive. The Miura, with its 4-litre V12, near-170mph top speed and utterly gorgeous lines by Marcello Gandini, was all of these things. But what's it like to drive?

The earliest P400 and P400S versions (the latter pictured here) were not without flaws, one being a propensity to take off as the Miura approached its maximum speed. The driving position's not the greatest, either. Anyone much over six feet will find their arms outstretched and their legs bunched up and splayed either side of the steering wheel. But the view out through the deep, wraparound windscreen and over those curving wingtops is ample compensation.

Prime the carburettors with a few quick pumps of throttle, then turn the key. The V12 stutters briefly before a quick blip

of throttle clears its throat with a blood-curdling shriek that's more racer than road car. The gearbox is initially reluctant to go into first and needs a calm but firm hand, the mechanism feeling delicate because of the wand-like gear stick, but also chunky because of the mechanicals below. The accelerator is beyond sticky, but then you're opening 12 throttle butterflies with a cable that loops and twists from the pedal to somewhere over your left shoulder…

Once you're up to speed and start to relax on open country roads, third and fourth are all you need and there's plenty of torque. The ride gives you confidence, the Miura feeling settled over bumps and cambers. Although there's really nothing over the front wheels, it's still a surprise that the steering is relatively light compared with the other controls. It's communicative, too,

the unassisted rim weighting and unweighting in your hands as you guide the nose accurately into a corner before metering out the throttle travel in jerky chunks, using the power to drive through and down the next straight. A firework of small explosions crackles from the exhaust when you back off.

It's the soundtrack that will haunt you forever. Explore the rev-range more thoroughly, accept that it does its best work beyond 3,500rpm, and you're in for an almighty treat. As speed rises, the shrill V12 takes on an altogether harder edge, overlaid by the howl from the transmission's straight-cut transfer gears. It's loud, but oh-so-musical. Potent, too. Only the hottest of today's hot hatches could keep up with a Miura in a straight line. And no modern car could ever melt your heart quite the way a Miura would.

1968

Ferrari *Daytona*

Ferrari's response to the Lamborghini Miura was an old-school front-engined super GT,
which was also the world's fastest production road car

SPECIFICATIONS

Years produced: 1968–73 **Engine:** V12, 4,390cc **Max power:** 352bhp @ 7,500rpm
Torque: 318lb ft @ 5,500rpm **0–60mph:** 5.9sec **Max speed:** 174mph
Price: £8,750/$20,000 new in 1968, £700,000/$900,000 today

Ferrari in the 1950s and '60s wasn't known for innovation – Enzo Ferrari himself was naturally conservative – so while Lamborghini started a revolution with the Miura, Maranello's riposte was a fresh evolution of its classic V12 front-engined berlinetta. The 365 GTB/4 (the Daytona name was coined later) was built around a magnificent quad-cam 4.4-litre V12, with a rear-mounted five-speed gearbox to keep the weight distribution as even as possible. It was a strict two-seater and clothed in slippery new bodywork, designed by Leonardo Fioravanti at Pininfarina. The combination was irresistible – it was independently clocked at 174mph, making it for several years the world's fastest car.

But the Daytona's reputation has suffered over the years, with many concluding that it is best viewed as a fast GT, only really suited to fast cruising. So what's the truth?

The interior is one of Ferrari's best, a winning blend of function and style, with a laid-back driving position, a full array of dials straight ahead and, of course, the classic open metal gate for the five-speed gearbox. The V12 engine is simply magnificent and offers a soundtrack to die for. And yet some people come away from a drive in a Daytona rather nonplussed. It's true that if you drive a Daytona cautiously, it feels rather heavy, cumbersome and uninspiring. The unassisted steering shoulders a lot of the blame for that, and the gearshift can be hard work, too.

It's only when you start to drive quickly – faster than you'd imagine you would in a 50-year-old 'classic' – that the whole car snaps to and starts paying attention. Suddenly the big Ferrari feels on its toes, beautifully poised. The heavy steering lightens up and you can now trim your line through a corner by foot as much as by hand. The sharp and snappy gearshift now makes sense and that engine – previously an oasis of wonder in a desert of disappointment – is now once more among like-minded friends.

The Daytona is a real driver's car, so if you're not going to really drive it, you'll be far better off leaving it parked. Drive it the way it wants to be driven and it will provide one of the greatest experiences of any Ferrari road car from any era.

SPECIFICATIONS

Years produced: 1969–74 **Engine:** V6, 2,419cc (246) **Max power:** 195bhp @ 7,600rpm
Torque: 166lb ft @ 5,500rpm **0–60mph:** 7.1sec **Max speed:** 145mph
Price: £5,485/$13,500 new in 1969, £350,000/$450,000

1969

Ferrari *Dino 206/246 GT*

Ferrari saw how many 911s were being sold by Porsche and decided it would like a slice of the action. The Dino was the result

Ferrari's first mid-engined road car wasn't, in fact, originally sold as a Ferrari at all. It was badged and sold as a Dino, after Enzo Ferrari's first son, to reflect how different it was from Ferrari's mainstream cars. In its original 206 guise, it had a tiny 2-litre V6 mounted behind, rather than in front of, the driver – both radical departures for Ferrari in the 1960s. But you only had to look at it and drive it to know it was every bit as special as any of the great berlinettas that came out of Maranello. It also seeded a whole genre of 'baby' Ferrari supercars that can be traced right through to today's F8 Tributo.

Settling behind the wheel of a 246 GT, you prime the three twin-choke downdraft Weber carbs with a few pumps of throttle. Then churn the starter with just the lightest pressure on the pedal and the V6 growls into life. No other car in the world sounds like a Dino, its voice rich, multi-layered. The spindly steel gear lever slots cleanly, away and back, into first. The clutch is ridiculously heavy, given how little work it must do, but it takes up the power smoothly.

You cruise at first, taking in the sights: the rising curve of the wings, the grouping of the eight beautiful Veglia dials and the unimprovable perforated Momo wheel. Compared with modern supercars, a well set-up 246 is gently suspended. Yet it never feels sloppy; it just breathes with the road, leaving pure feedback to reach your fingers. Time to wind it up a little. Second gear, 3,000rpm on the clock and let it go. The great surprise is that, despite having just 195bhp, it doesn't feel slow at all. There's a solid surge right away, the growl turning into a snarl.

In corners, the steering weights up almost immediately, becoming flooded with feel, and you can guide the nose into the apex with unwavering accuracy. The car is alive, on its toes, ready to change direction at zero notice. To guide a 246 through some curves, nowhere near the limit but just feeling it talk to you, is a rare and special experience. Of course, the Dino was a Ferrari, as much as any other and, what's more, better than almost all of them.

Datsun *240Z*

Datsun turned the sports-car world upside down when it launched the 240Z,

a thoroughly modern take on an old recipe

SPECIFICATIONS

Years produced: 1969–74 **Engine:** In-line 6-cylinder, 2,393cc **Max power:** 151bhp @ 5,600rpm
Torque: 146lb ft @ 4,400rpm **0–60mph:** 8sec **Max speed:** 125mph
Price: £2,288/$3,526 new in 1969, £25,000/$30,000 today

By the late 1960s, the British cars that had dominated the affordable end of the sports car scene for the best part of two decades were feeling their age. Cars like the MGB and Triumph TR6 were good-looking but their underpinnings were ancient. When Datsun launched the 240Z, it turned that cosy world on its head.

Its 151bhp straight-six beat the competition hands down. It was reliable and well-built. Its suspension setup – MacPherson struts at the front and trailing arms at the rear – is conventional by today's standards, but in 1969 this was state of the art for a mass-produced car.

The Z's proportions hinted at Jaguar E-type, but it was bang up-to-date, self-confident and clean-edged. And inside it's all sports car, too. The reclined driving position and upright wheel are standard fare, but the rest is a world apart from the trad British look. The one-piece dash is beautifully sculpted, and the bank of instruments set deeply within it clearly designed with the keen driver in mind.

Firing it up doesn't disappoint; the straight-six doesn't take much stoking and, after clearing its throat, it settles down to a rock-steady idle. Driving through town, the major controls all require effort – this was still a serious sports car. The throttle is long and linear, without a trace of stiction; the gearchange is quite heavy and deliberate; the clutch is meaty, the steering likewise.

On the open road, it all makes a lot more sense. As you plant the throttle in third at 50mph, the 2.4-litre straight-six picks up cleanly and the deep-chested, mid-bass roar from 3,000rpm is matched by purposeful acceleration, which still feels quick today.

The ride is knobbly on poor surfaces, but the damping is excellent, and when you hit country roads, the rack-and-pinion steering is full of feel. Its weight and gearing are spot-on and inspire confidence with smart turn-in and accurate response. It also helps that you're sat right back over the rear axle – an ideal situation for those with backsides tuned to identify the early onset of oversteer.

From the moment it hit the lucrative US market in 1970, the 240Z was a monster hit, selling over 40,000 cars per year. And since then the long-running line of Z-cars has totalled over two million in sales, becoming the most successful sports-car franchise of all time.

Range Rover

The original Range Rover brought 4x4s out of the fields and onto city streets and defined a whole new genre

SPECIFICATIONS

Years produced: 1970–96 (Classic) **Engine:** V8, 3,528cc **Max power:** 135bhp @ 5,000rpm
Torque: 185lb ft @ 3,200rpm **0–60mph:** 13.8sec **Max speed:** 108mph
Price: £1,998 new in 1970, £45,000/$58,000 today

On 17 June 1970, British Leyland's Range Rover was unveiled to an awestruck motoring press. The vehicle was revolutionary, innovative, modern and functional. Brainchild of engineer Charles Spencer King, the Range Rover sported David Bache-penned crisp good looks, aluminium bodywork, a mellifluous 3.5-litre V8, permanent four-wheel drive and tried-and-tested Land Rover off-road ability – and it combined all that with Rover motorcar levels of on-road comfort.

The Range Rover was a class act, but like the Mini, it was classless. Of purely functional design and fit for purpose, the Range Rover only became posh later on, when the middle classes realized they were the vehicle of choice of lords, lairds and landowners. The RR could be kept in Mayfair and was effective for whistling down the motorway to the estate at serious speed, where it could then be pressed into use off-roading on shoots or hunts.

Over the years, engines grew in size and output, the interiors became ever-more luxurious, and a four-door joined the range. But there's something appealingly pure about the original two-door, as the rapidly accelerating values of good-condition examples testify. To drive, however, it's very far removed from today's super-luxury SUVs.

The seats in these early examples were covered in vinyl, the idea being that the interior could be hosed out after a particularly heavy day on the farm. And talking of heavy, the four-speed manual transmission requires a fair bit of muscle, as does the steering, which, strange to tell, lacked power assistance on these early RRs.

Certainly the Range Rover is not the sort of vehicle you would naturally choose to hustle through central London but, once on the move, the steering lightens up appreciably, and while the gearshift is slow, it is cooperative, and the car's demeanour is friendly. Visibility is first class and the ride is supple. The all-round disc brakes work just fine, and you soon begin to lean the long-travel suspension into corners with more commitment while exploring the V8's torque-rich delivery. Not least, sitting up high with ample room and visibility, this is a comfortable place to spend time enjoying the traffic – as subsequent generations of 4x4 owners would go on to discover. But it was those early Range Rover adopters who experienced it all first.

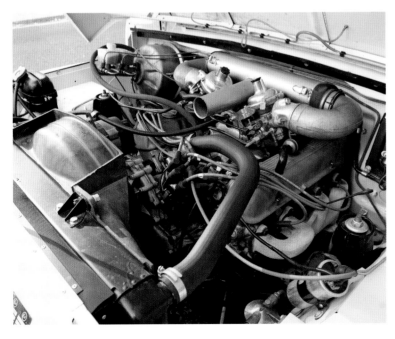

1970

Citroën *SM*

When Citroën built a GT, it was bound to be different. The SM was utterly original and featured a Maserati engine

This most majestic of *grandes routières* was a product of Citroën's brief ownership of Maserati. The Italian company provided the 2.7-litre V6 engine; the rest was pure Citroën. The glass front covered a sextet of Cibié lamps, the inner set swivelling with the steering. The entire body was highly aerodynamic, allowing the SM to slip to 135mph, and all in serene comfort thanks to the oleo-pneumatic suspension.

The same technology provided fully powered steering and brakes, too, the super-quick steering having just two turns between locks, while a rubberized floor-mounted button that responded to toe pressure, rather than movement, replaced the conventional brake pedal. In 1970, this was truly radical thinking and contemporary road tests often complained about the super-sharp steering and touch-sensitive brakes. Today we're more used to high levels of power assistance and, driven with understanding, the SM is utterly beguiling. You slide onto a soft leather chair that places you semi-reclined behind a small, fat-rimmed, single-spoke wheel and an array of oval instruments. Welcome to the future, 1970-style.

The quad-cam V6 engine, derived from the V8s that

Maserati originally developed for racing, has a wonderful bark, though you have to wind it up to 4,000rpm for it really to fly, and its note is slightly out of keeping with the SM's languid demeanour.

The light steering and progressive clutch make this a seriously simple car to drive away and feel comfortable in. The cylindrical gear knob is lovely but even better is the way the stick it's attached to slides between gears. It's creamily effortless yet mechanically direct in feel. And while the ride might be firmer than that of a DS, compared with all of its GT opposition, the SM is utterly cosseting.

Being a Citroën, and front-wheel-drive, this isn't a car you throw into bends – do so and it will lurch in the most undignified manner. Instead, feed it in with your fingertips, and feel the ample grip on fresh Michelin XWXs. Those used to more sporting GTs might find the amount of body-roll unacceptable, but the transition into roll is controlled and consistent. Eventually, you encounter a gentle understeer that's signalled by a squeal from the loaded front tyre. You'll need to be going pretty quickly to meet this point, so it's generally a good moment to back off – and savour a truly unique, and uniquely stylish, motorcar.

SPECIFICATIONS

Years produced: 1970–75 **Engine:** V6, 2,670cc **Max power:** 168bhp @ 5,500rpm
Torque: 170lb ft @ 4,000rpm **0–60mph:** 8.8sec **Max speed:** 135mph
Price: £5,480/$11,700 new in 1970, £50,000/$40,000 today

1972

BMW *3.0 CSL*

Once again, motorsport helped create a legend, this time in the outrageous shape of the CSL 'Batmobile'

SPECIFICATIONS

Years produced: 1972–75 **Engine:** In-line 6-cylinder, 3,153cc (Batmobile) **Max power:** 206bhp @ 5,600rpm
Torque: 215lb ft @ 4,000rpm **0–60mph:** 7.5sec **Max speed:** 138mph
Price: £8,000 new in 1972, £250,000+/$320,000 today (Batmobile)

In the early 1970s, BMW wanted to beat Ford in the European Touring Car Championship, so it created the 3.0 CSL, 'L' standing for *leichtbau*, meaning 'lightweight'. And light it was; in fact some 200kg/440lb lighter than the 3.0 CSi from which it was built. With it began a lineage of spectacular road-legal machines (and the birth of BMW's M Division) but none more spectacular than the CSL, especially when kitted out with the full aero addenda that earned it the nickname of the 'Batmobile'.

It was also spectacularly expensive – even the 'regular' CSL was £6,399 at launch in the UK, when an E-type Jaguar was £3,387. The Batmobile, complete with a larger 3,153cc motor and a decidedly un-road-legal spoiler sitting inside the boot, was a whopping £8,000.

Approach one today and you can't help but grin at the wings and fins (which were undeniably effective, as the 1973 Touring Car title proved), then you clink the little metal door handle open and slip into a shoulder-cut bucket seat that provides the perfect, suggestively laid-back 1970s posture. The motor takes a few seconds to fire, but does so cleanly and settles to a steady idle, thanks to the Bosch mechanical

injection. If you weren't already snared by the BMW 3.0 CSL, you will be now.

The leather-trimmed wheel is thin and delicate, and there's no slack at the straight-ahead. In fact the steering is comically heavy at low speed but all it takes is 15mph on the speedometer for the wheel to free up and provide the driver with an experience unavailable in any modern car.

Given that the power output is a modest 206bhp, it feels surprisingly lively. The immediacy of the throttle adds to the sensation of speed, but it also has heaps of torque and four gear ratios that could have been chosen for cross-country adventures. The gearshift is terrific – its lengthy action simply means you have longer to enjoy it. The car wants to rev, too: it pulls strongly from 2,500rpm, builds as generous helpings of induction noise blend into the cabin through 3,000rpm, then assumes a more aggressive tone all the way to 6,000rpm.

There's less grip than in a Porsche RS, so you apply small amounts of corrective lock at quite high speed, and all the while you're ensconced in the tiny bucket seat, afforded unrivalled visibility past the skinny pillars and using the wing-mounted strips to guide you.

1972

Porsche *Carrera 2.7 RS*

Another product of motorsport homologation, the 2.7 RS is quite simply one of the most intoxicating road cars ever built

T he defining 911 of its era, the 2.7 RS was designed for sub-3-litre GT racing, which meant building a minimum of 500 road cars. Within a week of the car's debut at the 1972 Paris Auto Salon, all 500 were sold. It would end up selling three times that number – a mixture of stripped-out Lightweight and slightly better-equipped Touring models – and go on to become the most coveted of all 911s.

So what makes it so special? With its wide track (it was the first 911 to have wider rear wheels than fronts), ducktail spoiler and Carrera script, it certainly looked the part. With its flat-six bored out from 2.4 to 2.7 litres, it made a solid 210bhp, and with extensive lightening – from thinner steel panels to ditching the rear seats – bringing the kerbweight down to under 1,000kg/2,204lb, this meant a killer power-to-weight ratio. Which meant 0–60mph in under 6 seconds. Best of all, though, is the way it feels.

The seats in this Touring version are sofa-squashy but seem to mould to you and prove very supportive. The upright windscreen frames a view of the slim wings gently dropping away and bending in towards the road ahead. All it needs is crosshairs… Twist the key and the flat-six settles to a reluctant, lumpy idle. Blip the throttle and the needle chases around the rev-counter with a hunger you don't expect. It sounds and reacts like a racer. The gearbox is a little notchy and imprecise; the floor-hinged pedals are a little tricky to get used to. The RS starts to challenge you immediately.

It feels supple even on ragged roads, front end bobbing gently over bumps. The engine feels keen and responsive, every extra centimetre of throttle travel rewarded with a firm shove in the back.

You feel your way into the grip levels, aided by unassisted steering of pin-sharp clarity, and lean on the traction afforded by the high-profile tyres a little harder on exiting each successive corner. The key is loading up the fronts as you turn in and utilizing the rear weight bias on exit. Just don't back off mid-corner… Stay committed and you feel the rear edging into an almost imperceptible slide. This picks up the inside front wheel, digging the outside tyre into the road and keeping everything neutral, with front and rear in perfect unison. Poise like this is timeless.

SPECIFICATIONS

Years produced: 1972–73 **Engine:** Flat-6-cylinder, 2,687cc **Max power:** 210bhp @ 6,300rpm
Torque: 182lb ft @ 5,100rpm **0–60mph:** 5.6sec **Max speed:** 150mph
Price: £5,825 new in 1972, £400,000+/$515,000+ today

1973
Lancia *Stratos*

It was rallying that spawned the Stratos, one of the most outrageous machines ever to wear number plates

SPECIFICATIONS

Years produced: 1973–75 **Engine:** V6, 2,419cc **Max power:** 190bhp @ 7,000rpm
Torque: 166lb ft @ 4,000rpm **0–60mph:** 6sec **Max speed:** 143mph
Price: £7,000 new in 1973, £450,000/$580,000 today

The Stratos actually started life as a 1970 concept car, the Stratos Zero, an outlandish wedge designed by Bertone's Marcello Gandini (who would go on to design a string of Lamborghinis). Lancia saw the potential for a bespoke mid-engined rally car and turned to Ferrari to provide the power in the form of the Dino's high-revving 2.4-litre V6.

Homologation for world rallying meant a minimum of 500 road cars. In fact only 492 were made before the rally car's frontline career ended, making the Stratos one of the rarest as well as most outrageous road cars of the era. And also, by reputation, one of the most challenging…

Inside, it isn't what you could call ergonomically sound. Adopting the bum-first, legs-next approach to entry and contorting yourself into place, the driving position is predictably skewed and you have no choice but to assume a long-arms, short-legs stance. Ventilation, meanwhile, is in short supply, the Perspex side windows juddering down in arcs. It's all very rudimentary.

Turn the key, listen to the fuel pump whine and, with a couple of throttle stabs, the transverse V6 fires with surround-sound fanfare. But, then, four chain-driven camshafts are spinning in their alloy heads just a few centimetres behind you. The dogleg gearbox feels baulky initially, the clutch on the heavy side, but once up and running the action is smooth and positive, so long as you remember to blip on down changes. The Stratos doesn't feel particularly fast by modern standards, but the sense of immediacy is striking.

The steering is light, but that's logical since there is little weight up front. Kart analogies are unavoidable, as it's incredibly precise, if perhaps a little edgy at speed. Get your gearchanges and braking finished before the corner, pick your line and the rest is done with the throttle. You can then call upon the fantastic traction to slingshot you out before savouring the choral backbeat on the straights. The sound of a Stratos nearing the upper end of its vocal powers is pure bliss.

As, indeed, is the sense of achievement when you overcome initial hesitancy and get it right. Stories of the Stratos's overabundance of power and shortness of wheelbase making it a white-knuckle ride aren't the whole story. You don't have to tiptoe – but to get the best out of one, you'll need to be pretty useful. There really is nothing else like a Stratos.

SPECIFICATIONS

Years produced: 1973–85 **Engine:** Flat-12-cylinder, 4,942cc (512 BB) **Max power:** 360bhp @ 6,200rpm
Torque: 330lb ft @ 4,600rpm **0–60mph:** 5.5sec **Max speed:** 180mph+
Price: £23,868 new in 1973, £300,000/$385,000 today

1973

Ferrari *Berlinetta Boxer*

Ferrari's first mid-engined flagship supercar was a landmark machine and certainly fast, if somewhat flawed

Ferrari had dipped its toe into mid-engined waters with the pretty little Dino, but the Berlinetta Boxer was its first full-on mid-engined supercar, replacing the front-engined Daytona as its flagship model. The engine itself was new, too, with its cylinders horizontally opposed (their action giving rise to the 'boxer' name). And it was all clothed in deeply attractive new Pininfarina bodywork. Ferrari fans had a new poster car, even if some road testers found the BB tricky at the limit. Initially launched as the 365 Berlinetta Boxer with a 4.4-litre engine, this grew to 5 litres for the 512 BB launched in 1976, an example of which is pictured here.

You drop down into the low-slung cockpit, where headroom is tight and the seating position almost fully reclined, the steering wheel a good stretch away and the pedals offset towards the centre of the car. The clutch requires a meaty shove and initially the cold gearbox oil makes the lever recalcitrant and sticky. So, slide it back into second through that exposed gate, then ease it forward into first and add some revs. Very soon you're savouring the unassisted yet pin-sharp steering and a wonderful sense of connection with the chassis

and drivetrain. It has that typical Ferrari mechanical tingle, and none of the controls has any slop whatsoever.

Onto the motorway, the BB strains at the leash. The flat-12 thrives on revs and has a wailingly crisp note at high rpm but, conversely, when you're cruising in fifth gear, it's surprisingly quiet and refined, while the suspension is both compliant and nicely damped. It's certainly no hard-core, tooth-rattling sports car.

And that notorious handling, said to be caused by the mid-mounted engine placement above the gearbox giving less-than-optimal weight distribution? On twisting roads, you can indeed feel it moving around on those rear tyres as the power comes and goes in a bend. If you unsettle it by lifting off after hurrying into a corner, you can feel the weight of the engine wanting to head off in its own direction behind you, but – at least on dry roads – it settles as soon as you reinstate power to the rear wheels. It's all pretty much as you'd expect with any mid-engined car. With the masses marshalled, working with you when you need them, the Boxer is a beguiling drive.

1974
Lamborghini *Countach*

Lamborghini gave the world the definitive supercar with its Countach,
but it took time for the reality to match the looks

SPECIFICATIONS

Years produced: 1974–90 **Engine:** V12, 5,167cc (5000 QV) **Max power:** 455bhp @ 7,000rpm
Torque: 369lb ft @ 5,200rpm **0–60mph:** 4.2sec **Max speed:** 190mph (5000 QV)
Price: £82,000/$100,00 new in 1985, £400,000/$515,000 today

he Miura may have been the first supercar as we know it, but the Countach defined the genre. With its claimed 190mph-plus top speed, Marcello Gandini-penned fighter-jet looks and upwards-opening scissor doors, it was a concept car made real. For a whole generation, this was the shape that got them hooked on cars.

Truth is, the first Countachs were cramped and underdeveloped and wouldn't get close to 190mph, though at least they didn't try to take off like the Miura had. For many, the 5000 Quattrovalvole (four valves per cylinder), introduced in 1985, is the sweet spot in the Countach series – faster and more capable than the early versions, and with space inside for grown adults, but without the OTT bodykit of the end-of-line Anniversary model. Those new cylinder heads and a capacity increase to 5,167cc lifted peak power to a very serious 455bhp and gave the Countach a top speed of 190mph, as verified by the UK's *Fast Lane* magazine.

The Countach still looks and feels outrageous today, even in a world seemingly awash with supercars. Getting in it means falling across the wide sill and into the single-piece driving seat, which forces you to adopt a reclined driving position. Flick the ignition, prime the fuel pumps for about 15 seconds, dab the throttle, then engage the starter. The V12 coughs, splutters… and, after a couple of blips on the pedal, explodes into life. Even at idle, it's loud and seriously addictive.

At low speeds all the controls are fearsomely heavy; the Countach only really comes alive at speed. On a motorway it will cruise brilliantly at 100mph, but the real fun is when you slot second and squeeze every last rev from the V12, right up to 7,200rpm, then repeat the process in third, before throttling back and listening to the exhaust's crackling firework display. And it really does feel genuinely fast. So much so that you have to plan ahead: it might have crushing straight-line pace, but it brakes like a 1980s car. Without a servo.

In tight corners the heavy steering makes it rather unwieldy. If you've the ability, it can be steered on the throttle but, again, the heavy steering means you need strong arms as well as quick wits to catch a slide. But on the right road, open and fast, there's very little to match the visceral thrills of a Countach QV.

1975

Porsche *911 Turbo*

The 1970s saw the first wave of turbocharged road cars, and leading the way was the 'whale-tail' Porsche 911 Turbo

If there's one car that embodies the potent myths and legends of turbocharged road cars, it's the original Porsche 911 Turbo. With its fat wheel arches, whale-tail rear spoiler and badass reputation for spitting reckless drivers off into the scenery, this late 1970s superstar still has a magnetism and charisma to make enthusiasts of a certain age go weak at the knees.

Drawing on Porsche's experience with turbocharged competition cars, the early 930-generation Turbo had a 3-litre single-turbo flat-six producing 260bhp and a four-speed gearbox (rear-wheel-drive only, of course). But that was just the warm-up act. The 3.3 that arrived in 1978 took peak power up to 300bhp, while work on the suspension was said to reduce its power-off tail-wagging tendencies.

The driving position in this 3.3 is excellent, though the floor-hinged pedals feel odd if you haven't driven an old 911 before. The long, wand-like gear lever has a protracted throw and a slightly notchy feel, but it has a sense of connection that matches the talkative (unassisted) steering.

The rear-mounted flat-six has a breathy, respiratory sound. It's smooth and sweetly responsive, but it takes a while for the boost to start swelling. Each of those four gears had a long stride by necessity, to reach all the way to 160mph. So wind it up in second gear and watch the speedometer needle sweep rapidly to just beyond 90mph. This is an effortlessly fast car, even today.

It copes with its prodigious pace, too. The suspension is soft, and when you're pressing on, you feel the nose begin to nod over undulations, but it never gets deflected from your chosen line. It turns in well, generating strong but soft-edged grip. Through corners, you learn to anticipate the turbo boost, pressing on the throttle a moment earlier than you would normally. Get it right and the Turbo squats onto its outside rear wheel, the tail *j-u-s-t* stepping out of line as boost builds, requiring only an instinctive smidge of opposite lock.

It pays to keep your wits about you, though. Get too greedy and the tail will kick wide more quickly and less progressively. Good fun in the dry, but a wet road demands circumspection. The Turbo's reputation is well deserved.

There would be many more generations of 911 Turbo in the years that followed, gaining four-wheel-drive and twin turbos as they went, but this is where it all started.

SPECIFICATIONS

Years produced: 1975–89 (930) **Engine:** Flat-6-cylinder, 3,299cc, turbo (3.3) **Max power:** 300bhp @ 5,500rpm
Torque: 304lb ft @ 4,000rpm **0–60mph:** 5.4sec **Max speed:** 162mph
Price: £23,200/$26,700 new in 1975, £100,000/$130,000 today

Volkswagen *Golf GTI*

When VW launched the GTI version of the Golf, it turned a compact hatchback into one of the most coveted cars on the planet

SPECIFICATIONS

Years produced: 1976–84 (Mk1) **Engine:** In-line 4-cylinder, 1,781cc (Mk1 1.8) **Max power:** 112bhp @ 5,800rpm
Torque: 109lb ft @ 3,500rpm **0–60mph:** 8.1sec **Max speed:** 112mph
Price: £4,705 new in 1976, £15,000/$19,000 today

hen the Golf replaced the Beetle in 1974, there were no plans for a sporty version. It was a small group of engineers and marketing men who came up with the GTI idea and built the first prototypes as an after-hours project, incorporating the fuel-injected engine from the then-new Audi 80 GTE. Fortunately, when they showed it to the management, they got a big thumbs-up.

When the Golf GTI went on sale in 1976, it wasn't just the peppy injected engine (originally 1.6, though later upgraded to a 1.8), the lowered suspension, wider wheels and ventilated disc brakes that made it cool. Red pinstripes, wider arches and a chin spoiler gave it real street cred. Suddenly this was the car to be seen in.

It still looks good today: foursquare stance, Pirelli P-slot alloys on this late 1.8 and that red stripe around the grille. And it's still a great little all-rounder, swallowing occupants and luggage, and able to cruise happily at an indicated 3,500rpm and 80mph. It's not fast by modern standards, but in its day there was enough punch to see off the more traditional sports car choices, and even today its 0–60mph in 8.1 seconds would match most 'warm' hatches. What's more surprising from a modern perspective is how smoothly the eight-valve four-pot revs, pulling with admirable strength all the way to the red line. Low weight helps: at 840kg/1,852lb, the GTI is 14kg/31lb lighter than a VW up!

On minor roads it really comes into its own, even when they're narrow, because so too is the Golf, and the view through its extensive fenestration means you can skim along millimetres from verges and hedges with total confidence. The steering isn't as precise or as wieldy as a modern hatch's – it's low-geared because there's no power assistance – but the upside is there's plenty of feel for the road. The brakes lack a modern car's bite too. So you drive the GTI in a completely different way from modern hatches: the emphasis is less on late braking, aggressive turn-in and encouraging the rear end to share cornering duties, and more on smooth inputs and maintaining momentum. Where no modern hatch can compete is in the sense of constant interaction. And they all owe a debt to their great-grandad, the original hot hatch.

BMW *M1*

In the late 1970s, BMW launched its first mid-engined supercar and the very first car to carry an 'M' badge

Long before it became a trim line on humdrum saloons and SUVs, 'M' stood for 'motorsport'. The earliest roadgoing M-cars were created by BMW Motorsport GmbH, the department that developed the company's competition cars – and the M1 was the very first.

It was conceived to be both the company's first mid-engined supercar and also a Group 5 contender in the World Sportscar Championship, though its racing career never really took off, mainly due to delays in development caused by partner Lamborghini dragging its heels. As a road-going supercar, it was subtle, beautifully engineered, refined and habitable, with a good turn of speed, thanks to its magnificent 3.5-litre 24-valve straight-six engine. But it was also expensive, and lacked both the outright firepower and the allure of a Ferrari or Lamborghini. Production ended after just 456 had been built, today making it one of the rarest and most coveted of all BMWs.

Its lines, the work of Giorgetto Giugiaro with input from BMW's Paul Bracq, still look fresh and modern. The cabin hasn't dated so well, and has a distinctly low-volume feel: the plain seats are squashy and the pedals offset strongly towards the centre of the car. But they often were in those days.

Twist the key and the fuel-injected straight-six churns slowly into life, almost as if it's on carbs; hook the dogleg first gear, find the clutch biting point and you're away. Quite quickly the M1 reveals itself to be light, tight and sweet, the twin-cam six super-smooth and really strong above 3,000rpm. It doesn't sound like an Italian supercar, the howl of the engine having a more classic tone, and by the same token it doesn't feel like one either; the unassisted steering is heavy but manageable and wonderfully precise, and the M1 feels poised and responsive, with a remarkably calm ride and a good match of power and grip. It feels polished and finely honed.

In its day it was as good as any mid-engined car from the supercar 'establishment' and it would also bequeath its superb straight-six engine to the first M5, the original super-saloon. But overall the programme was a painful experience for BMW. It would be many years before we saw another mid-engined Bee-Em.

SPECIFICATIONS

Years produced: 1978–81 **Engine:** In-line 6-cylinder, 3,453cc **Max power:** 277bhp @ 6,500rpm
Torque: 243lb ft @ 5,000rpm **0–60mph:** 5.8sec **Max speed:** 162mph
Price: £37,570 new in 1978, £650,000+/$670,000 today

1980

Renault *5 Turbo*

The combination of turbocharging and motorsport gave rise to some truly wild and spectacular road cars, none more so than Renault's bonkers 5 Turbo

SPECIFICATIONS

Years produced: 1980–86 **Engine:** In-line 4-cylinder, 1,397cc, turbo **Max power:** 160bhp @ 6,000rpm
Torque: 163lb ft @ 3,250rpm **0–60mph:** 6.6sec **Max speed:** 130mph
Price: £80,000/$100,000 today

R enault in the 1980s pushed its engineers to create cars that other manufacturers wouldn't even consider. This independent spirit was fuelled by a motorsport programme that saw the French manufacturer win at Le Mans, in Formula One and, in the case of the R5, on the stages of the World Rally Championship. And so it subjected its chic shopping hatch to an astonishing transformation, which turned it from a front-engined, front-wheel-drive hatchback into a rear-mid-engined, rear-drive monster.

The plan was to build the 400 road cars required by the rule book, but it eventually built 1,800. The first generation, know as the Turbo 1, had all the trick homologation parts, including lightweight aluminium roof and doors. The Turbo 2, built from 1983, was more conventional (and therefore less costly) in construction, if no less wacky in concept.

Open one of the T1's lightweight alloy doors and you gain access to possibly the wildest car interior ever to reach production: mad, modernist and minimalist in equal measure. By today's standards, the mechanical spec is rather feeble; an old 1.4-litre pushrod four delivering 160bhp, thanks to the

added puff of a large, laggy turbocharger. A kerbweight of just 900kg/1,984lb helps make the most of that, and in a funny way the lag that leaves you becalmed below 4,500rpm seems to intensify the rush when the boost gauge begins to twitch and you hear the engine fill its lungs.

It takes a while to dial yourself into the T1, but then you appreciate there's a harmony to the way it goes about its business. The steering is slow by modern standards, but it's in tune with the chassis, the rate of turn matched to the rate of roll so you don't upset the balance as soon as you turn the wheel.

You're always aware of the mass sitting behind you – much like in an old 911 – but, unless you provoke it, the T1 remains pretty benign. That said, a mid-corner lift of the throttle is enough to wag the tail, which would certainly temper your enjoyment (and commitment) on an unfamiliar road.

The driving experience is packed with quirks, but also with quality. Created by people who knew their stuff and understood how to get the best from a car, the Renault 5 Turbo 1 can truly be described as the genesis of Renault Sport's hot-hatch brilliance.

SPECIFICATIONS

Years produced: 1980–91 **Engine:** In-line 5-cylinder, 2,226cc, turbo **Max power:** 217bhp @ 5,900rpm (20v)
Torque: 228lb ft @ 1,950rpm **0–60mph:** 6.2sec **Max speed:** 144mph
Price: £32,995 new in 1989/$35,000 new in 1983, £40,000+/$45,000 today

1980

Audi *Quattro*

The Quattro redefined all-weather performance and turned Audi into one of the coolest brands on the planet

I f you were lucky enough to spend time in a 20v Quattro in the late '80s, it was an experience you would never, ever forget. The car was that good, that quick, that special. With its chunky looks and blistered wheel arches, the Quattro was also pretty much the coolest car on the road.

Even 30 years later, it doesn't disappoint, but it's not perfect. The driving position itself is a bit of a shocker, to be honest. The centre of the wheel is directly in line with the clutch pedal, so it feels a bit like you are driving the car from the wrong seat. But you can't help but smile the first time you twist the key in the ignition and the digital instruments light up in front of you, glowing red-on-black, much like a Casio watch from 1978.

Things get even better when you start driving, which in a 30-year-old car comes as a delightful surprise. The motor itself feels sweet as a nut, with a lovely smooth refinement to it on tick-over and a strange absence of the five-cylinder thrum you'd

expect. The 20v versions were always quieter, more efficient and, of course, more powerful.

In this day and age, 217bhp from a 2.2-litre five-cylinder engine is nothing special, but back then it was pretty tasty, and even now the 20v Quattro still feels decently brisk – and impressively lag-free – when you open it up. True, the clutch is ridiculously heavy and the gearchange is far too long-winded, but the way the 20v goes is still not to be sniffed at, especially between 2,000–4,500rpm, where it still feels genuinely potent. It steers quite sweetly, too, and goes round corners with a fair bit more precision that you might expect, even if it does feel its age when it comes to outright grip levels.

It still feels remarkably together, does the 20v Quattro. In fundamental terms, it is still a surprisingly well-sorted car, one that goes and grips and steers a whole lot better than a 30-year-old car should. And it still looks great after all these years. It's still cool.

1984

Ferrari *288 GTO*

As fast as it was beautiful, the GTO became an instant classic the moment it was unveiled

SPECIFICATIONS

Years produced: 1984–87 **Engine:** V8, 2,855cc, twin-turbo **Max power:** 400bhp @ 7,000rpm
Torque: 366lb ft @ 3,800rpm **0–60mph:** 4.8sec **Max speed:** 189mph
Price: £72,999 new in 1984, £2.5m/$3.2m today

When motorsport's governing bodies announced a new category, Group B, for racing and rallying, it pretty much gave manufacturers carte blanche to create the most advanced machines the world had yet seen, the only stipulation being that they had to build at least 200 road cars. Ferrari naturally embraced the new format and the result was the 288 GTO.

Superficially similar to the long-lived 308 GTB, it was actually pretty much new from the ground up. A tubular spaceframe replaced the 308's semi-monocoque. The body, featuring Kevlar and carbon fibre, was broader to encompass a wider track and fatter tyres, and longer in the wheelbase because the much-modified V8 engine had been turned from transverse to longitudinal, to accommodate twin IHI turbos, intercoolers and a new fuel injection system. With 110kg/242lb less weight to carry, and power up from 240 to 400bhp, performance was from another dimension.

The GTO still has the power to take your breath away, not least because the interior is quite luxuriously appointed: carpets, electric windows, classic perforated leather seats. It's clearly related to the 308, but no 308 ever went like this. It'll

fizz its rear tyres in first but thereafter remain remarkably well hooked-up to the tarmac, and it's so poised, so balanced, so easy to drive very quickly indeed.

It sails over tricky surfaces, barely acknowledging lumps and bumps that would be clearly felt in more modern supercars. And then there's the unassisted steering – direct, feelsome and marvellously weighted. Even on wet roads you can feel your way right up to the limit of the front tyres' grip.

The tougher the road, the better it gets, its twin-turbo V8 driving the tail into the tarmac and firing it up the road on a swelling, whooshing flood of torque. And if you ever get a chance to follow one that's being driven quickly, it's a spectacular sight into corners, round brake lights aglow, 2ft-long flames shooting from its blunderbuss-style tailpipes on the overrun.

We haven't even mentioned that the GTO is knee-wobblingly pretty and, with just 272 eventually built, much rarer than the F40 that followed. Politics meant it was never seriously raced, but Ferrari had created the ultimate road-going supercar of its day and one of the most beautiful of all time. No wonder it was – and remains – so desired.

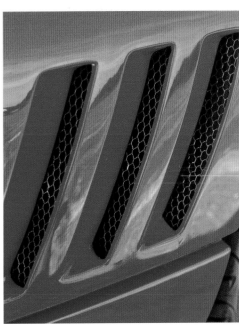

1984
Peugeot *205 GTI*

Peugeot raised the hot hatch to new levels of fun and excitement when it launched the 205 GTI

The Golf GTI had set the template, but it was the pretty little Pug that showed the world what riotously good fun an interactive little hatch could be. Power was only modest – just 105bhp from the original 1.6, a more impressive 130bhp when the 1.9 arrived in 1986 – though with only 850kg/1,874lb to propel and five tightly stacked gears, the performance was plenty lively enough. But it was the way it handled that really made the 205 stand out. It was as sharp as a blade – too sharp for some, who found its propensity for lift-off oversteer gave one or two unintentionally exciting moments.

Modern tyres have partly tamed that trait, but a 205 GTI still gets your heart pumping. Settling behind the thin-rimmed two-spoke wheel, the cabin feels airy, filled with light and devoid of thick, blind spot-creating pillars. It's also lacking any kind of air bag, ABS or stability control, and feels as robust as a Coke can.

On early cars the steering is unassisted, but once underway it's hyper-responsive and alive in your hands. You almost *think* it into corners, the smallest input bringing an instant change in direction. And there's not a hint of understeer, thanks to a rear end that comes into play the moment the nose begins to turn. It's a bizarre sensation, but if you can calm your initial inputs, the Pug flows beautifully. That first twist of lock is often the most you apply, for you instinctively unwind it almost as soon as you've turned in, abundant feedback from the wheel and seat telling you that the car has settled into a delicately poised tiptoe stance.

It's totally absorbing but it does come with a certain frisson of fear through long, fast corners, simply because the loaded steering is too heavy to have more than one stab at correcting any turn-in or lift-off oversteer. So it speaks volumes of the interactive nature of the 205 that you can leave a decent safety margin and still feel completely engaged in the action. And it gets better with every mile. The damping is great, the light gearshift fast and precise, even the brakes – usually the weak point on cars of a certain age – are more than decent.

There's purity here, a sweet balance of grip, grunt and stopping power harnessed by a live-wire chassis that feels sparkier than ever in an age of sanitized, dumbed-down machinery.

SPECIFICATIONS

Years produced: 1984–94 **Engine:** In-line 4-cylinder, 1,905cc (1.9) **Max power:** 130bhp @ 6,000rpm
Torque: 119lb ft @ 4,750rpm **0–60mph:** 7.9sec **Max speed:** 124mph
Price: £6,295 new in 1984, £12,000/$15,000 today

1986

BMW *M3*

The original E30-generation M3 delivered M Division goodness in a deliciously compact package

SPECIFICATIONS

Years produced: 1986–92 **Engine:** In-line 4-cylinder, 2,467cc (Sport Evo) **Max power:** 235bhp @ 7,000rpm
Torque: 177lb ft @ 4,750rpm **0–60mph:** 6.1sec **Max speed:** 154mph
Price: £22,750 new in 1986/$34,000 new in 1988, £100,000/$90,000 (Sport Evo) today

As we know, M stood for Motorsport, but most road cars from BMW's M Division were just that: designed and built for the road. The original E30-generation M3 was different, in that it was first and foremost a competition car, one that excelled on both racetracks and in rallies, and only became a road car to satisfy homologation requirements. So it really does have motorsport pulsing through it.

It looks so right too, crisp-edged, compact and purposeful, the 'box-flared' arches a functional necessity to clear its wider track, the rear screen more aerodynamically sloped compared with a regular 3-series. The mechanical spec doesn't look too promising on paper: a non-turbo four-cylinder engine, 2.3 litres in the early cars with a modest-sounding 212bhp, though the later Sport Evo had a rather more rousing 235bhp 2.5-litre unit. But, as with all the great cars, it's what it does with it that counts.

All E30 M3s were left-hand drive, so anyone used to right-hand drive will take a few minutes to acclimatize, particularly with the five-speed manual gearbox having first gear on a

dogleg, but it feels so right slipping into the sculpted seat and gripping the thin, suede rim of the steering wheel. The driving experience can be initially a little underwhelming. The steering has a relaxed feel; likewise, the suspension doesn't fidget or feel particularly alert. It's clear it's not going to offer up dynamic excitement unless you put in a bit of effort.

The first corner where an M3 clicks for you is a revelation. *Really* drive it and suddenly you don't notice the slowness of the steering, you simply enjoy the perfect weighting and a surprising keenness to turn in. The 48/52 per cent front/rear weight distribution gives one clue as to why it feels so good, so balanced, so biddable. The tail doesn't feel loose, it just follows, and the mass of the car seems concentrated low. There's also a fantastic suppleness to the suspension that lets the car breathe with the road, while the engine comes alive as you hold on to each gear and let it really sing.

In everything it does, there's a sense of purity, connectedness and mechanical honesty. Even more than the M1 and the mighty M5, this is the car on which the M Division built its reputation, its very essence.

1986

Ford *Sierra RS Cosworth*

This star of 1980s Touring Car racing also made a pulse-quickening road car – with wings on

SPECIFICATIONS

Years produced: 1986–92 **Engine:** In-line 4-cylinder, 1,993cc, turbo **Max power:** 224bhp @ 6,000rpm (RS500)
Torque: 204lb ft @ 4,500rpm **0–60mph:** 6.1sec **Max speed:** 154mph
Price: £19,950 new in 1986, £50,000/$64,000 (RS500) today

C ossie. It's more than 30 years since the legendary Ford first made its mark on the world's racetracks and rally stages, in the process spawning a series of wild and wonderful road cars, yet the name still resonates. All the road-going Cosworths were revered machines in their day, whether the early three-door or the later four-door Sapphire saloon, but the most coveted of all was the RS500, a true homologation special, of which just 500 were built. The output of the 2-litre turbo engine was upped from 204bhp to 224bhp, the block strengthened to cope with race levels of boost, and there was a larger intercooler too. The front bumper had extra cooling vents, while the huge rear wing got a more pronounced lip – and a second, smaller spoiler below it.

Even today it has an aura, an air of purpose that's only slightly dented by the cabin with its boxy shapes and truly terrible plastics, though it's partly redeemed by a pair of supportive and comfortable Recaro seats. The steering wheel looks huge and cheap but actually feels brilliant; likewise, the tall gear lever looks like a refugee from a Transit van but moves around the five-speed gate with surprising precision.

The Cosworth YBD motor catches with a fruity *bwaarrp*. The clutch has a slightly sharp bite, but the steering and brakes both impart plenty of confidence-inspiring feel. That engine is hilariously laggy, though – you squeeze your foot down, then a bit more, and a bit more still before the Garrett turbo finally begins to spool and force some life into the power delivery. Given some fast, open roads, however, and above 4,000rpm the note hardens as boost builds and there's a real rush of power to compensate for the low-rev torpor.

Dynamically, the RS500 is old-school: modest grip levels, but plenty of feel and transparent handling traits. The steering is power-assisted but there's a decent weight to it, and the rate of response strikes a sweet balance between agility and stability. As you'd imagine, it will oversteer with provocation, and the transition from grip to slip can be swift on wet roads. Balancing the slide requires delicate throttle work. In fact, in the rain the spiky power delivery can easily overwhelm the rear tyres, even in a straight line in third gear. It certainly guarantees you give the Cossie your full attention. But then you'd expect nothing less.

1987
Porsche *959*

Porsche poured everything it knew into the 959, the most advanced supercar the world had yet seen

SPECIFICATIONS

Years produced: 1987–88 **Engine:** Flat-6-cylinder, 2,849cc, twin-turbo **Max power:** 444bhp @ 6,500rpm
Torque: 369lb ft @ 5,000rpm **0–60mph:** 3.7sec **Max speed:** 197mph
Price: £155,266 new in 1987, £1m+/$1.3m today

The 959 was Porsche's riposte to Ferrari's 288 GTO. Like that car, it was inspired by the short-lived Group B regs in motorsport, but in most other ways it couldn't have been more different. Where the GTO married visceral pace to classical beauty, the 959 was a technological wonder.

The twin-turbo flat-six engine in the tail had its roots in Porsche's Le Mans racers but used sequential turbos to counter the dreaded throttle lag of forced induction. The 959 had permanent four-wheel-drive with multiple driver-selectable modes, the torque split front-to-rear governed by a computer-controlled multi-plate clutch. The suspension damping and the ride height were both adjustable from the cockpit. The highly aerodynamic bodywork used aluminium and Kevlar to reduce weight. The top speed of 197mph was then the fastest ever seen from a production car.

It still looks sensational today, like a future vision of a super-911. The interior is slightly disappointingly like a 911's from the same period, and when you first set off, that's how it feels, too. You've got the same airy feeling in the cabin, with great visibility all round, and despite the greater breadth of the Kevlar bodywork, it feels positively small in modern traffic.

Initially, it doesn't feel any more potent than a regular 911 either. But at around 4,500rpm, everything changes. The soundtrack switches to something much louder, deeper and all-consuming, the roar filling the cabin – and you're launched down the road at a mind-boggling rate. Snatch the gear lever straight back into third and the 959 continues to charge forward until the first corner appears and you need to lean on the decently reassuring brake pedal.

The steering is slightly inert around the straight-ahead, but as soon as you turn into the corner and load up the surprisingly soft suspension you get more feedback. There's a huge amount of grip available and after a while you find yourself slinging it into corners and getting on the power much earlier than you'd ever dare to in a 911 from the same period. As confidence increases, you feel the nose pushing a fraction; a little lift tucks the front wheels back on line, and if you've got space, you can open the steering a bit and keep feeding the power on until it drives the rear round a little more.

But it's the 959's power delivery that makes the biggest impression. Once experienced, never forgotten.

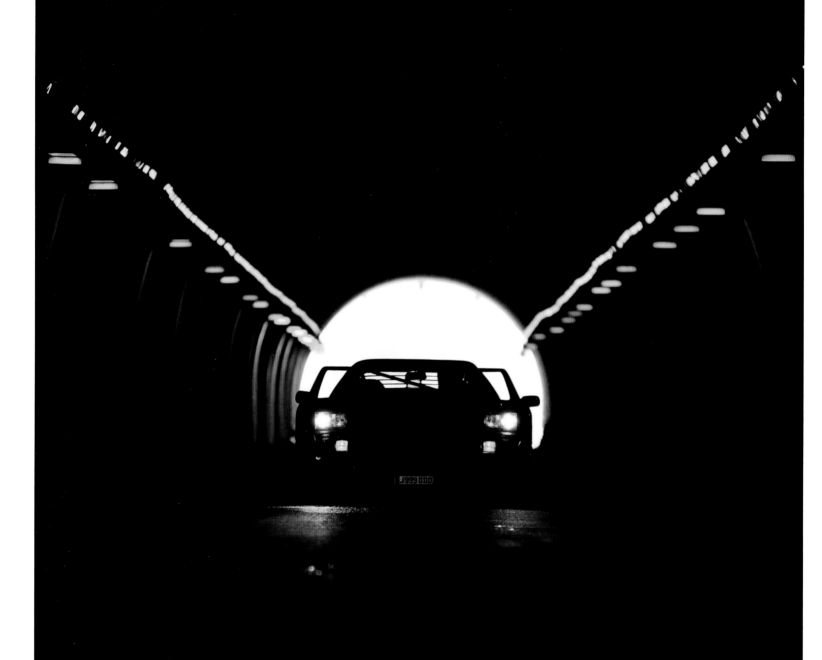

Ferrari *F40*

Porsche's claim to the world's fastest car didn't last long;
the F40 was the first production car to break the 200mph mark

SPECIFICATIONS

Years produced: 1987–92 **Engine:** V8, 2936cc, twin-turbo **Max power:** 471bhp @ 7,000rpm
Torque: 426lb ft @ 4,000rpm **0–60mph:** 3.9sec **Max speed:** 201mph
Price: £193,000/$395,000 new in 1987, £1.25m/$1.1m today

Work on a successor to the 288 GTO, to take on Porsche's 959 in Group B, was well advanced when the motorsport authorities decided in 1986 to can the category amid fears over rising speeds and rising costs. Ferrari simply developed the GTO Evoluzione further into what would become the F40 – and, in the process, created one of the most savagely fast and charismatic road cars there has ever been. The '40' referred to Ferrari's 40th year, in 1987. That Maranello was able to claim a top speed of 201mph and hence steal the world's fastest car title back from Porsche made it all the sweeter.

The F40 used an enhanced version of the 288's twin-turbo V8, enlarged to 2,936cc and with the wick turned up to give a stupendous 471bhp at 7,000rpm, and none of the 959's fancy four-wheel drive and programmable damping; there wasn't even power assistance for the steering. Inside, it's as Spartan as any supercar has ever been, with bare floors and exposed carbon fibre, so you're completely focused on the driving. And focused you must be…

Clamber over the carbon sill, drop into the red cloth bucket seat, heave the clutch pedal to the floor, twist the small key and press the squishy black rubber starter button. The V8 catches

almost instantly, settling to a busy idle. The open-gated dogleg gearshift requires a firm hand and the steering at low speed is so heavy that you reach to the top of the wheel for extra leverage. The engine gives you little at low revs, but as you accelerate, you hear the boost building, the pent-up energy gathering, then suddenly, at 4,000rpm, the boost hits the rear wheels and all hell breaks loose. With only 1,100kg/2,425lb to propel, the 426lb ft punch in the back is gloriously unsettling and you're struggling to find a stretch of road long enough to unleash it properly, and each time the boost dies there's a sound like the sea crashing on a shingle beach.

Slowly your legs become used to the pressure they need to exert on the pedals, and your forearms tense hard as you grip the small wheel in bends as you muscle the front Pirellis into corners. And as you put in the effort and gradually increase the speed, so it starts to come alive and make sense. You cannot be timid with an F40. Be respectful but don't be fearful, because if you're not on top of it, then it will feel like the car is driving you.

There's virtually no roll, so every input commands a direct response. But the V8 needs to be anticipated. Even if you drop down to dogleg first for a hairpin, you need to be back on the throttle much earlier than you expect. Get it right, though, and it's huge fun riding this wave of escalating boost, any initial understeer switching very quickly to oversteer. It's controllable oversteer, the stiff rear end reacting instantly to opposite lock, turbos keeping the rear wheels spinning beautifully as long as you don't panic and jump out of the throttle. In fact, the F40 up on its toes, boosting hard, sliding sideways on the exit feels happier than at almost any other time.

Driving an F40 quickly is physical and involving and awkward and rewarding all at once – and there will always be moments when it is magnificently intimidating – moments through quicker corners, when the chassis is loaded and the engine is climbing through that transitional 4,000rpm and you realize you're holding your breath.

Lancia *Integrale*

An Italian exotic masquerading as a family hatchback – that was the rally-bred Integrale

The Integrale was, quite literally, shaped by rallying. To stay at the head of the field, it evolved constantly over its long lifespan, developing increasingly more blistered arches to cover its wider track, bigger wheels to provide more grip and accommodate bigger brakes, and extra bulges, wings and vents to keep everything cool in the heat of battle. It was crushingly effective. Taking over the Quattro's mantle, it won six successive World Championships between 1987 and 1992. That pedigree, combined with its chunkily purposeful looks and the ability to hunt down a Porsche 911 on a demanding road made the 'Grale a cult favourite with fans of fast road cars.

The ultimate – and the most sought-after today – is the Integrale Evo. It still oozes purpose and aggression, and it still quickens the heart rate as you settle into the deep embrace of the seat, run your hands around the rim of the delicious, three-spoke Momo steering wheel, and eye the prominent boost gauge. And that's despite its 2-litre turbocharged four producing what is by today's standards a very modest 215bhp.

That engine, you quickly discover, is loaded with character – sweet and smooth but conspicuously turbocharged,

it makes the surge after 4,000rpm all the more exciting. It's matched to a chassis of remarkable pliancy, and the light-on-its-feet Lancia manages to combine tiptoe agility and four-square grip seamlessly. You don't actively look to unstick the 205-section rubber, as you might in a Mitsubishi Evo, but instead drive within the Integrale's elastic, easy-going limits. It dances over rough surfaces, while the sharp steering response tells you the tyres are keyed-in and working hard, helped no doubt by quite high levels of body-roll.

For raw pace, the Integrale was quickly eclipsed by the next wave of turbocharged 4x4s, but there's real detail in the quick steering, great feel through the brake pedal and the chassis is keen and forgiving – so long as you don't let it fall into the clutches of understeer. It has fantastic traction, plenty of soft-edged grip and a keen, torquey engine. Coupled with compact dimensions and a confidence-inspiring level of stability when you do breach its limits, the Lancia makes the most of everything it's got and still feels genuinely rapid.

As an all-weather, all-road 'affordable supercar', the Integrale had more style and panache than any other car of its era.

SPECIFICATIONS

Years produced: 1987–94 **Engine:** In-line 4-cylinder, 1,995cc, turbo **Max power:** 215bhp @ 5,750rpm (Evo II)
Torque: 229lb ft @ 3,500rpm **0–60mph:** 6sec **Max speed:** 137mph
Price: £25,000 new in 1987, £45,000/$58,000 today

Mazda *MX-5*

In 1989, Mazda reinvented the classic, affordable sports car –
and enthusiasts the world over took it to their hearts

SPECIFICATIONS

Years produced: 1989– **Engine:** In-line 4-cylinder, 1,597cc **Max power:** 115bhp @ 6,500rpm
Torque: 100lb ft @ 5,500rpm **0–60mph:** 9sec **Max speed:** 114mph
Price: £14,249/$13,800 (Mk1) new in 1989, £2,000+/$6,800 today

That the MX-5 was inspired by 1960s British sports cars was hardly a secret. The Lotus Elan-like body with its pop-up headlights, the exhaust note tuned by Mazda to mimic that of old Triumph TRs and MGBs... It sought to recapture what people remembered motoring being like: freedom and fun, deserted roads, carefree attitudes. Mazda took all that and then rose-tinted it with reliability.

The modest specification seems like it was from another age, too: just 1,597cc, four cylinders, 115bhp, five-speed manual gearbox, rear-wheel drive, double-wishbone suspension at all four corners, tiny wheels with 185-section tyres, and a kerbweight of just 971kg/2,141lb. It was designed to evoke the joy of motoring in its simplest and most uncomplicated form – and a well-preserved Mk1 is still an absolute hoot 30 years later.

0–60mph was never what the MX-5 was about. Narrow, twisting roads are its natural domain, and the steering gives you all the accuracy you need to thread the car inch-perfectly. It rolls a little in the corners and its tyres have plenty of give in their tall sidewalls, but once it's settled into a turn, you can adjust its attitude gracefully. String several corners together and it flows continuously as it delicately transfers its 971kg/2,141lb from left to right. There isn't really the power to work the rear tyres very hard (unless it's wet) yet still all four are involved as the balance reacts to lifts of the throttle or dabs of the brake or changes of lock. The engine, meanwhile, gives its modest power willingly, while the gearshift is a snickety joy, with a tight action as it positively releases from one ratio then equally positively slots into the next across the short gate.

On the sort of roads where the MX-5 excels, you might not top 60mph all day. That might sound boring, but it isn't, and that's the magic of the little Mazda – in all its generations. Speed is not always the answer, and on roads like these what is required is poise, a small footprint and not a lot else. In a world where authorities seem to want to strangle the speed of cars more and more, it's a philosophy that has become ever more relevant.

SPECIFICATIONS

Years produced: 1989–2002 **Engine:** In-line 6-cylinder, 2568cc, twin-turbo **Max power:** 276bhp @ 7,000rpm
Torque: 289lb ft @ 4,400rpm **0–60mph:** 4.8sec **Max speed:** 165mph
Price: £50,000 (R34) new in 1989, £50,000+/$65,000 today

1989
Nissan *Skyline GT-R*

It was nicknamed Godzilla, and it went from racetrack to cult road car, destroying any competition that got in its way

T he GT-R originally earned its hero status on the racetrack, but it was the *Fast and Furious* film franchise that helped the cult of the GT-R grow to global proportions. That, and the attentions of the tuning industry, which extracted massive power from its twin-turbo straight-six engine. It had the chassis hardware to handle it, too, with ATTESA four-wheel drive and Super HICAS four-wheel steering. No wonder the motoring press nicknamed it Godzilla.

Even in standard trim, as with the end-of-line R34 version shown here, it was an extremely rapid machine. Indeed, road testers often expressed scepticism that the GT-R had only 276bhp as standard (the ceiling agreed between carmakers in Japan at the time). It always felt a bit more like 300-plus.

That competition-hardened straight-six under the long bonnet is an engine with character in both sound and delivery. It's not like other turbo units, lacking the immediate, small-throttle response of today's light-pressure turbo engines, but also being unlike early turbos, with their eye-widening, blue-touch-paper delivery. It builds more like a naturally aspirated engine, with not much up to 3,000rpm and growing enthusiasm thereafter. You can hear and feel the boost arriving, the loping, gravelly growl of the straight-six swamped by the hiss of air being ingested, compressed and fed into the engine. As the revs march evermore confidently upwards, the engine finds its voice again and its delivery grows and expands its impact until you're at 6,000rpm and the car's surging forward.

The weighting and feel of all the major controls – the gearshift, pedals and steering – are in harmony. The shift of the six-speed Getrag gearbox is particularly delicious. There's a sweet, biddable balance to the handling, too. The fact that you can't feel the rear steering counter-steer on the way into a corner (aiding turn-in) and quickly switch to parallel steer (to restore stability) is a big compliment to the engineers. Then there's the all-wheel-drive grip. Nail it out of a roundabout and there's a bit of squat and absolute traction.

On low-grip surfaces it becomes distinctly rear-drive, but in a friendly way. Nissan's V-spec cars like this one have an active rear diff and only when this can't find enough grip at the rear tyres to deploy the torque does drive head to the front. It's still deeply impressive – and monstrously good fun.

Lamborghini *Diablo*

The Countach's replacement was every bit as dramatic and, as the '90s dawned, it re-embedded Lamborghini in the supercar hierarchy

T he Countach was some act to follow, but Lamborghini pulled it off with the Diablo, another slice of wild, V12-engined exotica from the drawing board of Marcello Gandini. And if the early examples could be a challenge to drive, with a rather crude feel and heavy controls (unassisted steering on the first generation), by the time the 6.0 VT appeared, the Diablo had matured into a worthy successor. With its power steering, four-wheel drive and improved quality thanks to new parent company Audi – and even more power from the biggest version yet of the Lambo V12 – this was a Lamborghini as you'd hope it would be.

It still has the power to take your breath away. It's still an event just to be around, and it gets the heart thumping just pulling that scissor door shut and churning that mammoth V12 into life. Audi's money meant the engine had been treated to variable valve timing and completely new calibration, which made it a puppy-dog at low revs but allowed it to remain a salivating psychopath at the top end.

Of course, you don't just jump into a Diablo and drive it quickly; it takes a while to acclimatize to the driving position, the bizarre dash architecture, the way the wheel reaches way into the cabin space, the lack of rearward vision – and the sight of the flared-out rear hips in the mirrors causing you to hold your breath when you pass oncoming traffic. You feel like the captain of a 737, right at the pointy end of a vast machine.

The manual gearbox is a peach, the clutch a brute. But, of course, it's the engine that dominates at first – and what really impresses is its appetite to work and rev. Where a Ferrari 575's V12 becomes breathless at the very top end, the Diablo 6-litre keeps pulling.

And then there's the 4WD system, one that gives a driver confidence in the wet, and yet still leaves the car feeling rear-driven under normal conditions. And when you eventually get past the initial intimidation and make the required leap of faith, you find you can drift wide on the exit of turns. Do that and you'll be in awe of its inherent balance. It's a reminder that the Diablo is – like all the best Lamborghinis – first and foremost a great driver's car.

SPECIFICATIONS

Years produced: 1990–2001 **Engine:** V12, 5,992cc (6.0 VT) **Max power:** 550bhp @ 7,100rpm
Torque: 457lb ft @ 5,500rpm **0–60mph:** 3.8sec **Max speed:** c.200mph
Price: £155,000/$239,000 new, £150,000+/$190,000+ today

1990

Honda *NSX*

Exquisitely engineered and wonderfully usable, the NSX instantly made traditional supercars feel stroppy and highly strung

SPECIFICATIONS

Years produced: 1990–2005 **Engine:** V6, 3,179cc (3.2) **Max power:** 276bhp @ 7,300rpm
Torque: 224lb ft @ 5,300rpm **0–60mph:** 5.7sec **Max speed:** 168mph
Price: £55,000/$60,000 new in 1990, £45,000+/$65,000+ today

Knowing Ayrton Senna was involved in its development always gave the NSX extra cachet, but it was undeniably special at the time, proving that an exotic mid-engined sports car didn't have to be temperamental or tricky to drive or to see out of. The all-aluminium NSX was a car you could use every day. Everything about it was as slick and finely honed as any other Honda, which certainly gave traditional supercar makers like Ferrari food for thought.

The first cars had 3-litre engines with a very modest 252bhp; the later 3.2 saw that rise to the 276bhp limit agreed by Japanese carmakers at the time, but even today an NSX has an aura about it that elevates the car above its less-than-jaw-slackening power, torque and performance figures.

The interior is a mix of Japanese executive chic and impressive simplicity. The view out is beautifully clear, the wheel-arch tops rising helpfully into view. It really is so easy to simply get in and drive.

The suspension is supple. Actually, it's borderline soft, but there's damping control to go with the comfort. The steering – power-assisted in this 3.2 – has a slightly slow-witted rate of response that mirrors that of early non-assisted cars. It forces a less-than-urgent driving style on you, but this smoothness actually makes a refreshing change and tallies with the 'everyday' mission statement.

As you'd expect, the engine and gearbox play a starring role. In fact, they are spectacularly impressive. Honda's jewel of a V6 always felt stronger than the spec sheet suggested, and that feeling holds true today. It has such class, from the silken refinement and appetite for revs to the steely howl that grows in intensity until, just when you think it can't feel or sound any better, the VTEC (variable valve timing and lift) kicks in and the NSX reveals its alter ego. The gearbox is a perfect partner, with a clean, rapid shift and a tight, precisely honed feel.

Overstep the limit of grip and, if the back end builds momentum, it can be quite tricky to catch, so you tend not to drive it like that, revelling instead in its supple chassis and superb powertrain. Perhaps it lacks the visceral appeal of an Italian supercar, but its style of delivery and quality of engineering are right up there with the very best.

1992

Mitsubishi *Lancer Evo*

Born for the rally stage, the Lancer Evo made a compelling road car,

and the Tommi Mäkinen edition was the best of the lot

SPECIFICATIONS

Years produced: 1992–2016 **Engine:** In-line 4-cylinder, 1,997cc, turbo **Max power:** 276bhp @ 6,500rpm
Torque: 275lb ft @ 2,750rpm **0–60mph:** 4.6sec **Max speed:** 150mph
Price: £32,995 (Mäkinen) new in 1992, £30,000+/$38,000 today

The Evo's ten separate evolutions spanned a remarkable 24 years and, while the technology became ever more sophisticated, the basic recipe stayed the same throughout: a rally special built around the Lancer saloon, with a four-cylinder 2-litre turbocharged engine and rugged four-wheel drive. The boxy lines, plasticky cabin and the fact there's a mere 2-litre 'four' under the bonnet might lead you to wonder quite why the Evo became a cult car – even when it's the limited-run Tommi Mäkinen edition pictured here, named after the four-time world rally champion. When you first drive off, the oddly weighted and feel-free steering just around the straight-ahead only serves to further furrow your brow.

But as soon as you've felt the way a Mäkinen's front end dives for a corner, there is no doubt. Now the steering is brimming with feedback and the whole car is so keen to dart one way or another that it feels positively buoyant on the road surface, almost to the point of flightiness. Trust the grip and soon you find you can take what would be liberties in almost any other car. The way the Evo leans on its outside front tyre

and seems to hoick its inside rear wheel in the air gives a perfect picture of the grip available. Soon, the way you can actively and aggressively use the weight transfer becomes riotously good fun.

Feel the front end push and you sense the Mäkinen is all done. But keep on the power and the four-wheel-drive system and AYC (Active Yaw Control) rear differential feeds the outside rear wheel with more torque, the understeer magically evaporates and the car adopts some angle at the rear.

It's a spooky but hugely exciting feeling and from here on in it's as if you've got the Evo on a string. Keep your foot in and the angle will stabilize and you'll rocket out of the corner; lift sharply to loosen the rear grip and further rotate the car.

This car's appetite for being driven with abandon is deeply infectious. The gravelly 276bhp engine loves to rev-out, the tyres howl but never truly give up, the brakes have real bite and feel, and the chunky, unburstable five-speed gearbox is joyous when hurried. Tommi Mäkinen's wild-eyed commitment was legendary and this car has the same unswerving focus.

1992

Subaru *Impreza WRX*

The flat-four-engined Impreza was the Evo's rival in rallying and on the road –
and rarely better than in its two-door P1 form

SPECIFICATIONS

Years produced: 1992– **Engine:** Flat-4-cylinder, 1,994cc, turbo **Max power:** 276bhp @ 6,500rpm
Torque: 260lb ft @ 4,000rpm **0–60mph:** 4.9sec **Max speed:** 150mph
Price: £37,847 (P1) new in 1992, £20,000+/$26,000 today

J ust as with Mitsubishi's Evo, there have been many generations of the Impreza WRX and a bewildering number of different versions within each generation. You'd need the rest of this book to cover them all. But, again, they all followed a very similar basic format – though in the Impreza's case the motive force is a low-slung 'boxer' turbocharged flat-four engine. It's what gives every Impreza its distinctive, pulsing voice.

The Prodrive-developed P1 shown here used the same four-wheel-drive system and turbo engine, but in a limited-edition two-door version with the wick turned up to 276bhp, ready to compete head-on with the ultimate Evos of the day, including the Mäkinen edition.

Right away, it feels special. It's easy to look at the humble origins of the Impreza and fixate on the prosaic elements, like the dash. But when you're actually driving the car, all you can see are the big bold bonnet scoop through the windscreen and the enormous rear wing in the rearview mirror – hardly everyday sights.

Likewise, the gloriously rich, warbling exhaust note is as distinctive and iconic as any 'thoroughbred' sports car.

Your torso is gripped snugly by a Recaro seat, the gearshift is short, quick and pleasingly mechanical. The steering feels a little slow-witted at first, but after just a couple of corners you realize that it's well matched to the amount and rate of roll in the suspension.

The more challenging the road – the more it ducks and dives through crests and compressions, the more the tarmac has been gouged by engine sumps – the better the P1 gets. Damper technology has advanced in the last 20 years, but the P1 has a suppleness and compliance that lets it work beneath you. Even when there's air under one or more of the wheels, it still feels calm and controlled.

Turn in hard and you feel the relatively skinny front tyres scrub wide quite early, but it's almost immediately followed by a gentle transition into a neutral or even mildly oversteering balance. As the focus shifts to the outside rear tyre, you invariably find you're on the throttle early and hard, driving the P1 out on a surge of boost and burble. The flat-four punches out every bit of its 276bhp, too. It's no wonder these cars developed – and continue to have – a devoted fanbase. The people's champions.

McLaren *F1*

The F1 was so beautifully engineered, so uncompromising, so fast, that the benchmarks it set would stand for decades

W hen you drop into the F1's central driving seat – always from the left-hand side, to avoid snagging yourself on the gear lever – there's a lot to take in, not least the glorious, panoramic view through the windscreen. But it's the details that provide endless delight: the ignition key that slots into the chassis plate; the unassuming red starter pip, hidden beneath a flip-top guard; and the smooth, spherical gear knob that fills your right palm perfectly.

Don't waste your time looking for the Sport button or the damper settings or even traction control because there aren't any. Nor is there any power assistance for the steering or the brakes. This is a car in which you have to configure your head to suit the car, not vice versa.

Twist the key 90 degrees clockwise, listen to the buzz of solenoids and pumps, then press the little red button. After the briefest of click-whirrs from the starter motor, Paul Rosche's V12 masterpiece awakens and, after clearing its throat with a sharp pulse of revs, settles to a busy, superbike-like idle.

The V12's urgency is the stuff of legend. Its sharpness and ferocity are sensational, each millimetre of throttle travel yielding mighty, perfectly metered force. As for the noise it makes, well, it's 30 per cent Stradivarius, 70 per cent wild, carnivorous animal.

Each gearchange requires sharp, positive inputs, but you can't just smash it through. It needs guiding if you're to avoid getting tangled on the way across the gate. The steering

SPECIFICATIONS

Years produced: 1993–98 **Engine:** V12, 6,064cc **Max power:** 627bhp @ 7,500rpm
Torque: 479lb ft @ 4,000–7,000rpm **0–60mph:** 3.2sec **Max speed:** 240mph
Price: £540,000 new in 1993, £10m+/$12.8m+ today

weight is a bit of a shock, especially in tighter bends, but when you're up and running, most corners are dispatched without needing to work the wheel more than half a turn. The upside of the physical effort is that it serves to heighten the experience, for it magnifies the feel, precision and perfectly judged rate of response.

In slow corners you can lean on the front end until you feel the nose just begin to run wide. Through faster corners you need only small squeezes of lock, coaxing the F1 to follow your chosen trajectory. What you can't do is take liberties. You need to be aware of cambers, crests, surface changes and lingering patches of damp that might upset the finely balanced division of labour between the rear Michelins.

Once you've applied some steering lock, felt the front end work towards its limit of grip and the body begin to roll as lateral loads increase, you soon learn that an additional squeeze of throttle will readily break traction out of slow

corners. The first time that happens triggers an involuntary spasm of fear, but the abundant torque means you can keep the rear wheels over-rotating at modest revs and throttle openings, so it's not the knife-edge process you'd imagine. But you do need to be smooth and swift when unwinding the lock.

Things are different at higher speed, but understand that 25-year-old supercars prefer not to be asked more than one question at a time and then all will be well. Drive it like a Nissan GT-R and there's a very real chance you'll be ruining your underwear and your insurance underwriter's year.

The truly remarkable thing about the F1 is just how far in advance it was of every other supercar when it was launched. In recent years we've seen pretenders, but never anything you could describe as a credible rival. Faster and more powerful? Yes. More flamboyant? Certainly. But more complete? More pioneering? More engaging? More pure? Never.

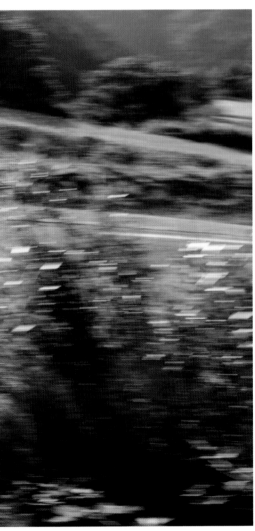

SPECIFICATIONS

Years produced: 1993–96
Engine: In-line 4-cylinder, 1,988cc **Max power:** 148bhp @ 6,100rpm
Torque: 126lb ft @ 4,500rpm **0–60mph:** 7.6sec **Max speed:** 134mph
Price: £13,275 new in 1993, £4,000–£8,000/$5,000–$10,000 today

1993
Renault *Clio Williams*

The Williams elevated the hot hatch to a new level – and it was the seed for generations of Renault Sport hotshots to come

ontroversy stalked the Clio Williams, as it often does with icons, automotive, human or otherwise. Initially built to allow Renault to take its hatchback rallying, the Williams was to be sold in a limited run of 3,800, each wearing a numbered plaque. Enthusiasts, some with an eye for an investment, loved it. But then Renault couldn't resist building a new batch…and then another…In all, 12,100 examples were eventually built. Owners of the originals kicked up a stink, and Renault lost a lot of goodwill.

But what's remembered today is just what a cracking little car it was – and still is. The first hot hatch to put the legendary Peugeot 205 GTI in the shade, it also inspired generations of rapid Renaults, including the similarly iconic 182 Trophy.

The 'Williams' bit was to capitalize on Renault's link with the F1 team; the uprated engine grew from 1.8 to 2 litres compared with a regular Clio 16v; there was a beefed-up five-speed gearbox and stiffened suspension with a wider track and slightly wider wheels, too. It was a thorough job.

The engine dominates at first. There's a harmonic in the mid-range that sends a fizz through the shell, and an under-bonnet chuckle on the overrun, reinforcing the notion that this is a tiny car with a mightily powerful engine. It revs out raucously and keenly, but it's the mid-range muscle that makes it – the ability to snap forward at 3,000rpm.

Its power-assisted steering has surprising weight for anyone weaned on modern machinery. It's not a car you drive just from the wrists; you work the wheel, moving your grip to feed the car into a corner. This is also precisely the moment that the Williams truly comes alive.

Its approach to enthusiastic cornering almost exclusively involves just three wheels. The fourth – the inside rear – gets a welcome respite, and hangs for a fleeting moment in thin air. It's masterfully effective, forming a stable platform from which the car can summon terrific grip and poise.

The Williams demands to be driven with a joie de vivre that strikes right to the core of what driving for fun is about. Even today, it's able to accelerate, brake, turn and corner at a level that's not far off the current crop of superminis. In 1993 it must have been a thing of wonder.

1994

Audi *RS2 Avant*

Combining Porsche's know-how with Audi's dominant quattro hardware, the RS2 ignited

a desire for absurdly rapid estate cars

SPECIFICATIONS

Years produced: 1994–96
Engine: In-line 5-cylinder, 2,226cc, turbo **Max power:** 315bhp @ 6,000rpm
Torque: 302lb ft @ 3,000rpm **0–60mph:** 4.8sec **Max speed:** 163mph
Price: £45,705 new in 1994, £25,000/$32,000 today

I t was Ferdinand Piëch, head of Audi's supervisory board in the early 1990s, who hit on the idea of getting Porsche to help develop Audi's first super-estate. And it really was a joint venture. Viewing an RS2 today, it's staggering just how many bits were shared with contemporary Porsches.

The wing mirrors, the front bumper with its indicators and sidelights, the five-spoke 17-in Carrera Cup wheels…look closer still and you see that the brake calipers actually spell it out for you with the seven white letters on a red background.

Porsche badges also greet you when you lift up the bonnet. It's Audi's 20-valve in-line five-cylinder turbo engine, but for the RS2 it got hotter camshafts, a 30-per-cent bigger KKK turbocharger, new Bosch engine management, new injectors, freer-flowing exhaust and a bigger intercooler. The end result was 315bhp at 6,500rpm and 302lb ft at 3,000rpm.

Twist the key and it comes to life with a dry, high-pitched clearing of its throat before settling to a bassy but relatively demure idle. On the move, the ride is quite firm, so it's a surprise when the RS2 rolls quite a bit in corners, while the steering is weighty but rather lacking in feel. The grip really

does feel unimpeachable, though, even under fairly severe provocation with the throttle. You don't get the lovely mild-oversteer balance that the best four-wheel-drive performance cars excel at, but the Torsen (torque-sensing) quattro system is hugely impressive through faster corners, the car leaning more than expected but also displaying real tenacity.

There isn't much going on low down in the engine's rev-range. The party starts to get going at 3,000rpm but it only really delivers its full punch from 4,000rpm. It's a very old-school turbocharged power delivery, and that certainly makes it exciting. Road testers recorded 0–60mph in 4.8sec, which made the RS2 faster than every contemporary Porsche bar the Turbo. Interestingly, the official time of 5.4sec was conveniently slower than every contemporary Porsche.

So even though it's not quite as satisfying to drive as the Porsche badges would lead you to hope, it did start our love affair with unnecessarily powerful estate cars. The RS2 oozes exclusivity and instils a lust in people that very few cars, and even fewer estates, ever have. For that reason, it will always remain a legend.

1995

Honda *Integra Type R*

A quarter of a century after the Datsun 240Z was unveiled, Honda launched a
Japanese performance coupé for a new era: the DC2 Integra Type R

SPECIFICATIONS

Years produced: 1995–2000 (DC2) **Engine:** In-line 4-cylinder, 1,797cc **Max power:** 187bhp @ 8,000rpm
Torque: 131lb ft @ 7,300rpm **0–60mph:** 6.6sec **Max speed:** 145mph
Price: £19,500 new in 1995/$23,100 new in 1997, £10,000/$13,000 today

You accelerate gently at first, the engine whirring, curiously toneless. Change into second at maybe 4,000 and press your right foot down with more intent. The same mechanical whirr, now increasing in volume and intensity. By now your foot is pressing the slim pedal into the carpet, ready for the point when the yellow needle is just shy of 6,000…

As the higher-profile cam lobes come into play, the engine changes. Buzz makes way for yowl, induction roar bursting through the firewall like it's rice paper. And still you're nailing that right-hand pedal, keeping one eye on the tachometer…7,000, 8…finally slicing into third just before the rev-limiter calls time at 8,700rpm. Few cars with this cylinder count have an engine so intoxicating.

Honda's transformation of the DC2-generation Integra from runabout to road-racer was astonishing: reinforced suspension towers and sub-frames, extra spot-welding between panels, thinner glass, the removal of soundproofing, lightweight alloy wheels, and a close-ratio five-speed gearbox with a helical limited-slip differential. The four-cylinder, 1.8-litre engine was hand-built and hand-finished, with polished intake ports, high-compression pistons, balanced crankshaft, wider, 62mm throttle body and, of course, those high-lift, high-duration camshafts actuated by Honda's VTEC system.

The ride on modest wheels and tyres isn't harsh, with the grip perfectly matched to the performance. And every control seems calibrated to give its best when you put in the effort. Throttle response is unremarkable at low revs but Sabatier-sharp with the needle standing to attention, the gearshift never better than when it snicks through the gate at maximum attack.

The Type R's true genius is revealed in a sequence of long, fast corners. You're working the engine harder than ever and the brakes as little as you dare, feeling the tyres bite consistently at every corner. The car tips into a curving right with the high-lift cams working away in third. The nose remains locked to its line, but as the speed climbs, the steering lightens just a fraction. It's not understeer, but a subtle, delectable few degrees of rotation at the rear axle, helping align those four headlights with the front tyres, and the Type R exits the corner all-square just in time to grab fourth.

It's been lauded as the greatest front-wheel-drive car ever, but that undersells it. The Integra Type R ranks as one of the truly great driver's cars of any kind.

1995

Ferrari *F50*

How do you follow an icon like the F40? With a V12-engined F1-inspired hypercar
that's even more of a blast to drive

SPECIFICATIONS

Years produced: 1995–97 **Engine:** V12, 4,699cc **Max power:** 661bhp @ 8,000rpm
Torque: 347lb ft @ 6,500rpm **0–60mph:** 3.7sec **Max speed:** 202mph
Price: £342,700/$475,000 new in 1995, £2m/$2.6m today

Few cars from any era have made the connection between motorsport and road cars quite so brilliantly as the F50. Its 4.7-litre 513bhp V12 was derived from a genuine Formula One engine. That engine formed a load-bearing part of the car's structure – common in Formula One, almost unheard-of in a road car. The tub – the main structure – was fully carbon fibre. The spring/damper units were inboard-mounted and operate by pushrods, again just like in an F1 car. It was also the last Ferrari 'hypercar' with the classical open-gate gearshift, and no traction control, power steering or anti-lock brakes. The result was a machine that involved, challenged and rewarded like few others before or since.

That V12 barks into life and idles with a glorious, deep, hollow howl, the whole car trembling – a reminder that the engine is bolted directly to the carbon tub. Indeed, everywhere you look in the cockpit is glossy carbon fibre. Moving off, there's quite a commotion as the 60-valve V12 climbs the lower slope of its torque curve, every shade of vibration discernible through the seat of your pants, yet the ride is surprisingly supple.

Ease the firm throttle down an inch or so and the car snaps forward instantly, the V12's note deepening and hardening, the effect magnified by the F50's light build (only a little over 1,200kg/2,645lb). Beyond 4,000rpm it suddenly hits its stride, the delivery ramping up in urgency like some sort of mega-Honda-VTEC engine, complete with an incredibly rich, spine-tingling note. And the gearshift is just sublime – as precise, perfectly weighted and mechanically satisfying as you'd hope.

At first the steering feels weighty, the brakes rather numb, but at speed there's real agility and poise, with a stream of detailed feedback that allows you to push hard and know just how hard you're pushing. It's beautifully balanced, a smidgen of understeer letting you know you've got it loaded, and if the engine's in its sweetest spot, between 6,000 and 8,000rpm, you can neutralize it with a measured amount of throttle so that the F50 feels right on its toes.

The faster you go, the more mesmerizing it becomes. It bombards you with information and demands your total attention without ever becoming recalcitrant and tiresome, the steering filtering out everything you don't need to know and amplifying the important stuff.

Of all Ferrari supercars, the most engaging – physically and emotionally – is the F50.

Lotus *Elise*

The Elise was a lightweight revelation in 1996, redefining Lotus. And more than two decades later, the recipe still feels deliciously right

Lotus was in the doldrums by the mid-90s. Its aging Esprit supercar was on borrowed time; its entry-level front-wheel-drive Elan had failed to set the world alight. The Elise changed all that, winning massive critical acclaim and converting a whole new generation of drivers to the joys of low weight and a brilliantly involving chassis. The key was a bonded aluminium structure that was both strong and light, and the sheer genius of the car's ride and handling. The Elise brought magical dynamics to the mainstream.

Over the years there have been many different versions, different powertrains, trim levels, special editions, but those key ingredients are still the heart of its appeal. To drive any Elise is to be beguiled by the connection between driver and machine, and between machine and tarmac. And that's just as true whether it's an early Series 1 with just 118bhp or a Series 3 supercharged car like the one in the photos with a rather more potent 217bhp on tap.

Driving this 2012 Elise is a welcome reminder of why enthusiasts fell so in love with the delicate little Lotus. You drop down into the embrace of the seat, surrounded by the aluminium tub, the spartan ambience focusing all your attention on driving. Right from the off, it's fun, intimate and involving, and as you gather speed, you hear every bit of road grit pinging off the underside of the car, while the unassisted steering lightens beautifully and responds to the most delicate inputs.

The supercharged Toyota engine in this car has a beefy mid-range but it likes to be revved, its buzz-saw bark sweeter with the roof off, providing the perfect soundtrack. But what really stands out is the clarity of feedback you get from the car and the accuracy with which you can place it on the road, even when driving close to its limits. As you steel yourself to brake later and carry more speed into corners, you enter that magical zone where the car seems to dance through the twists and turns, working all four corners in harmony with the road.

Pretty soon, all the cares of the world melt away, your senses fully engaged in the process of threading this fizzy little sports car down a twisting road. Almost a quarter of a century on, there's still nothing quite like it.

SPECIFICATIONS

Years produced: 1996– **Engine:** In-line 4-cylinder, 1,798cc, supercharger (S) **Max power:** 217bhp @ 6,800rpm
Torque: 184lb ft @ 4,600rpm **0–60mph:** 4.5sec **Max speed:** 145mph
Price: £36,200 new in 1996, £20,000+/$26,000 today

1998

BMW *M5 (E39)*

BMW practically invented the supersaloon with the first M5 in the mid-'80s, but the best of them all
was the late '90s E39, one of the truly great M cars

SPECIFICATIONS

Years produced: 1998–2003 **Engine:** V8, 4,941cc **Max power:** 394bhp @ 6,600rpm
Torque: 369lb ft @ 3,800rpm **0–60mph:** 4.8sec **Max speed:** 155mph (limited)
Price: £59,995 new in 1998/$69,400 new in 2000, £40,000/$40,000 today

There have been a number of fine M5s over the decades, but the E39 generation was an absolute sweet spot, when all the stars aligned to produce a car that was stupendously quick but beautifully rounded in character, deliciously tactile and subtly stylish. Its brawny V8 had bags of torque and real soul, and there weren't too many electronic gizmos to get in the way of the driver's interaction with the machinery: among its many attractions, the E39 was the last M5 to feature a manual gearbox before the now-ubiquitous paddles took over.

It's a wonderfully discreet package, the sober lines, heavily dished rear wheels and quad tailpipes (which would become an M5 signature) only hinting at the potency beneath. Inside, there's a fundamentally sound driving position and white-faced dials that are a model of clarity. The 4.9-litre V8 fires up with a rich rumble, and as you move away the gearshift is a little notchy, though this improves with speed and a positive hand.

It's a heavy car at 1,700kg/3,748lb, but the wonderfully smooth, free-revving engine is more than up to it, while the chassis controls the bulk with remarkable precision, the M5 feeling lithe and agile in a way you just don't expect. What's more, a skilled driver will have a ball getting the rear end mobile and balancing the slide on the throttle.

It's not completely analogue. There are the early stirrings of the configurable electronics that will insulate the communicative abilities of later M cars. Here it's just one button, labelled 'Sport', giving sharper throttle response and an extra dollop of steering weight – not particularly big or clever but, as with so much else about this M5, very nicely judged. Likewise the suspension: conventional springs and dampers tuned for a perfectly brilliant ride/handling compromise – brilliant because it combines great comfort with almost absurdly exploitable driftability (once you've switched off the one-stage traction control), ensuring that driver and passengers are kept equally happy, though not necessarily at the same time.

Anyone who has driven an E39 M5 will agree that it represents a high point in the development history of the fast saloon car. While subsequent M5s and their rivals have become faster and cleverer, none of them delivers the rounded experience of the E39.

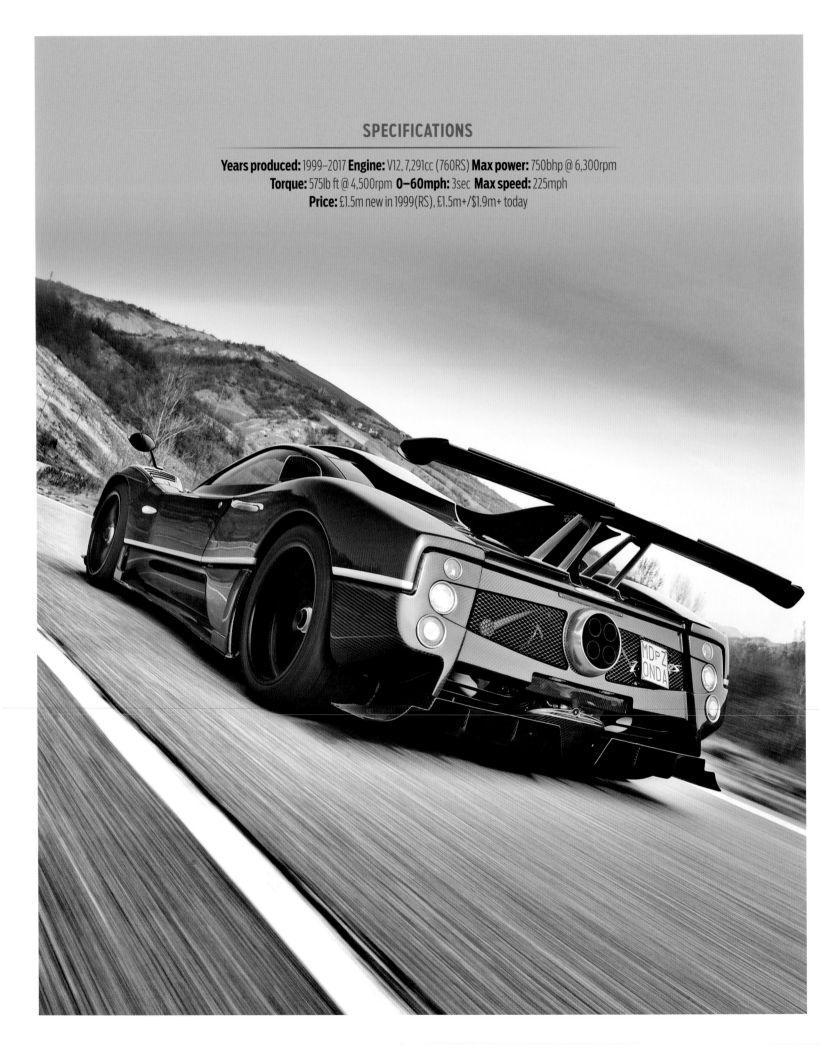

SPECIFICATIONS

Years produced: 1999–2017 **Engine:** V12, 7,291cc (760RS) **Max power:** 750bhp @ 6,300rpm
Torque: 575lb ft @ 4,500rpm **0–60mph:** 3sec **Max speed:** 225mph
Price: £1.5m new in 1999(RS), £1.5m+/$1.9m+ today

1999

Pagani *Zonda*

Pagani burst onto the supercar scene in 1999 with a car so astonishingly good it rocked the supercar establishment to the core

The Zonda was the brainchild of Horacio Pagani, an Argentine-born ex-Lamborghini engineer who reckoned he could build something even more thrilling, even more exotic than Ferrari and Lamborghini – and he succeeded in the most spectacular fashion imaginable.

Carbon fibre was Pagani's speciality, and the Zonda was positively dripping in the stuff, to the great benefit of weight – and hence performance and handling. The original car had a modest-sounding 389bhp from its bought-in Mercedes V12, but the outputs rose quickly as Mercedes agreed to supply bespoke engines from its AMG performance division. By the time this ferocious 760RS version arrived in 2012, peak power was up to a formidable 750bhp (760PS, hence the name) and the top speed had climbed to 225mph.

The RS was a roadgoing version of Pagani's track-only Zonda R and was nicknamed La Bestia, or The Beast. Clothed in bare carbon fibre with matt-black wheels and the most radical aerodynamic addenda ever seen on a Zonda (or just about any road car), it certainly looks the part. The black Alcantara-covered bucket seat beckons you to climb over the chunky sill, its carbo-titanium weave glinting in the sunshine. A press of

the scarlet button near the gear selector and that 7.3-litre V12 snorts into life; flick the right-hand paddle to select the first of the seven gears in the automated manual gearbox and you're away, warily at first, acutely conscious of the 2m-/6½ft-wide bodywork.

With a dry weight of just 1,210kg/2,668lb, the 760RS boasts a power-to-(dry)-weight ratio of 630bhp per ton. The acceleration, at any speed, is instant and eye-widening. It is a staggeringly powerful engine. Yet even though this is the most extreme of the breed, the qualities that make all Zondas such a joy are all present. The ride remains exemplary, completely defying your expectations for something that is so low it appears to be glued to the tarmac. And while the engine is rabid at the top end, there's still a truckload of torque at any revs. No matter what gear you're in, the acceleration is never less than ferocious.

Yet it's the howl that accompanies each serious prod of the accelerator that's truly shocking. Mix the heavy snarl of a Ferrari V12 with the wail of a wrung-out superbike and you'd be only halfway to the full-blooded battle cry of the Zonda, the quad exhausts crackling with every downshift. Pure theatre.

Ariel *Atom*

At the turn of the century, track days were booming. Cue one of the wildest road-legal machines the world had ever seen

SPECIFICATIONS

Years produced: 2000– **Engine:** In-line 4-cylinder, 1998cc, supercharged (3.5R) **Max power:** 350bhp @ 8,400rpm
Torque: 243lb ft @ 6,100rpm **0–60mph:** 2.6sec **Max speed:** 155mph
Price: £64,800 new in 2000 (3.5R), £30,000+/$39,000 today

It was a young British design student, Niki Smart, who came up with the concept for the Atom with its radical 'exoskeleton' and exposed cockpit. Engineer and senior lecturer Simon Saunders liked it so much that he put it into production and a new British sports car maker, the Ariel Motor Company, was formed. Across the following two decades, the Atom has been refined, gained ever more power, spawned an all-terrain version called Nomad, and blown away everyone who's ever strapped themselves aboard – including Jeremy Clarkson, whose face memorably distorted during a particularly frenetic track test on *Top Gear*.

The Atom's performance jumped into the hypercar league in 2014 with the 3.5R, which had a supercharged Honda engine pumping out a cool 350bhp and driving the rear wheels via a six-speed paddleshift sequential gearbox. In a car weighing just 550kg/1,212lb, the resulting power-to-weight ratio of 647bhp per ton was a match for any Italian or German supercar of the day and – in the context of the minimalist Atom – rather more exciting.

Swing your left leg over the fat tubing that forms the side structure of the chassis while holding the roll bar for balance, then pop your right leg in and drop down into the moulded seat. No car gives you a sense of exposure like an Atom, yet few deliver such a sense of strength and security, either. Flick a few toggles, push the starter button and the Honda motor kicks into life just behind your shoulders. You use the clutch to pull away and for downshifts, but once you're on it, upshifts with paddles are clutchless, so the rush is unrelenting.

Big throttle openings elicit the most sensational noise – a kind of sped-up, serrated whine like a bench saw cutting through steel. There's a great induction roar, too, and with each 40-millisecond downshift a solitary high-velocity gunshot report leaves the tailpipes.

The shock and awe of the 3.5R's performance is truly remarkable, but so, too, is the balance and poise of its chassis. At first everything feels overly urgent, but if you can relax your shoulders, arms and wrists and let the car talk to you, the edginess fades and you find it's every bit as drivable and playful as a Caterham Seven. For those who want the biggest road-legal buzz, the supercharged Atom delivers an experience like no other.

2000

BMW *M3 (E46)*

A second M3 entry in the Dream 100 may sound like an indulgence, but the E46-generation M3 CSL
was a very special machine

SPECIFICATIONS

Years produced: 2000–07 **Engine:** In-line 6-cylinder, 3,246cc **Max power:** 355bhp @ 7,900rpm (CSL)
Torque: 273lb ft @ 4,900rpm **0–60mph:** 4.8sec **Max speed:** 155mph (limited)
Price: £58,455/$45,400(CSL) new in 2000, £50,000+/$35,000+ today

he E46-generation M3 that arrived in 2000 was a fine machine, but three years into its production run BMW gave M-car fans something really special. Resurrecting the iconic CSL name, it took the basic M3, added more power while subtracting weight, thanks to liberal use of carbon fibre – even the roof was made of the glossy black stuff – fitted sticky semi-slick tyres and turned the attitude and the soundtrack up to 11. Here was an M3 with real edge – and a fast-appreciating collector's piece today.

Slip into the tight embrace of the race-style seat, survey the swathes of carbon fibre, take hold of the slim, suede-covered steering wheel rim and the CSL instantly feels a cut above other M3s. There's more menace and purpose to the note of the straight-six, too, thanks in large part to the addition of a carbon-fibre airbox. Press the Sport button and it sounds even better, with a complex, almost metallic timbre that makes you feel you've got half a V12 in front of you.

That button simultaneously sharpens the throttle response of the wonderfully potent, naturally aspirated straight-six, which feels good for every one of its 355bhp.

The SMG paddleshift gearbox is nowhere near as smooth as modern dual-clutch transmissions, but it fits the character of the CSL perfectly, too, especially when you're really 'on it', the rapid-fire gearshifts perfectly in tune with the road-racer vibe.

The chassis is fabulously direct without being nervous – imagine the agility of the E30 M3 in a slightly bigger, heavier package. Riding on slightly less extreme Goodyear Eagle F1 tyres compared with the original track-day spec Michelin Cups, it's firmly suspended, yet it never feels harsh and jarring. Its steering is a revelation, too: light but brimming with deliciously resolved feel and not one millimetre of wasted motion. Turn and the CSL changes tack instantly – no body roll, seemingly no suspension-bush compliance to blur the message, just lightning responses, terrific precision and masses of grip. And yet you can adjust its cornering balance on the throttle, which makes it great fun, too.

Almost 20 years on from the original E30 M3, the M3 E46 CSL showed that BMW's M division could still recapture the old magic, add an extra layer of performance and create another instant classic. No wonder those values keep rising.

Lotus *Exige*

Looking all the world like a baby Group C racing car, the Elise-based Exige was confirmation that Lotus built the purest driving machines on the planet

SPECIFICATIONS

Years produced: 2000– **Engine:** In-line 4-cylinder, 1,796cc **Max power:** 192bhp @ 7,800rpm (S1)
Torque: 146lb ft @ 5,000rpm **0–60mph:** 4.6sec **Max speed:** 136mph
Price: £31,471 new in 2000 (S1), £40,000+/$52,000 today

The Exige name has been around for two decades now and has graced a series of the most brilliantly focused closed-top sports cars. The recent Exige Cup 430, with its 430bhp V6, shows that the flame burns as brightly as ever – a track-biased hard-core road-racer that's as intense a four-wheeled experience as it's possible to imagine and probably the ultimate expression of the lightweight line that started with the Elise way back in 1996.

But to experience the Exige in its purest form, you need to go back to the original, Series 1 car, launched in 2000. Clearly directly descended from the Elise, it used the same bonded aluminium tub and naturally aspirated Rover K-series engine but here, in highly tuned 192bhp VHPD (Very High Performance Derivative) form, enough to punch the flyweight Exige from 0–60mph in 4.6sec.

While the bodywork again was clearly related to the Elise, the Exige really did have the pocket Group C racer vibe down to a tee. It was a miniature exotic, pert and purposeful – and it's every bit as alluring today as it was 20 years ago. The only part that's not terribly tempting is the small, shallow aperture that's revealed when you open the door. Once you've managed to post yourself through the letterbox, you find yourself cocooned in a beautifully uncluttered cockpit, aluminium and Alcantara trim continuing the road-racer feel, the lack of distractions leaving you free to concentrate on the driving.

At whatever speed you're covering the ground, the weighting of the unassisted steering constantly and subtly fluctuates at the rim of the tiny steering wheel. The engine needs to be kept above 5,000rpm to be on the boil, but the delicate gearshift is better than its remote linkage suggests, and the extruded aluminium pedals are perfectly placed, so snicking between ratios is easily done. Accelerating hard, the 192bhp VHPD four-cylinder fills the sparse interior with a hollow, blaring bark.

Jinking through a series of turns, the little Exige has huge reserves of grip to lean on, yet the kerbweight of just 780kg (1,720lb) combined with Lotus's renowned chassis tuning skills means that at times it seems to be almost floating down the road. The short wheelbase means you can place the Exige wherever you want, scribing precise lines through bends, and yet you can adjust your trajectory with a lift of the throttle without feeling you're about to spin. Bliss.

Lamborghini *Murciélago*

The replacement for the Diablo was every bit as spectacular, and in the LP670 SV

the old-school Lambo reached its absolute zenith

SPECIFICATIONS

Years produced: 2001–10 **Engine:** V12, 6,496cc (LP670 SV) **Max power:** 661bhp @ 8,000rpm
Torque: 487lb ft @ 6,500rpm **0–60mph:** 3.2sec **Max speed:** 212mph
Price: £221,335/$274,900 new in 2001, £140,000+/$182,000 today

No supercar maker does street theatre quite like Lamborghini, and a Murciélago never fails to turn heads or draw a crowd wherever it parks, even before the signature Lambo scissor door swings skywards. And never more so than in hard-core LP670 SV form with its fizzing orange paintwork and jutting carbon-fibre wings and splitters. This was the ultimate expression of the traditional Lamborghini supercar, the underpinnings of which had their origins in the Countach, powered by the ultimate version of the seemingly immortal V12 engine that could be traced all the way back to the very first Miura.

With lashings of carbon inside and out, the SV was lighter than other Murciélagos, and more powerful, too, the 6.5-litre V12 pumping out 661bhp. To feel the full effect, you need to find a longish, straight road, select third gear and, loping along at tick-over, floor the throttle. That epic engine snaps you forward instantly, initially churning out a low, heavyweight pulse that ripples through your soft tissue. It then evolves, becoming lighter and more urgent until, at somewhere between 5,000 and 6,000rpm, the fizzing fuse hits the kegs of gunpowder. *Pow!* The engine note loops upwards and the SV lunges forward, covering the last couple of thousand rpm so quickly that the first few times you're too late to prevent it battering the limiter.

There's a rather old-school feel to the rest of the SV – the automated single-plate clutch is rather clunky if left to its own devices and simply brutal in Corsa mode, while the steering's weighting is definitely on the beefy side. It's not as composed or ultimately as quick across the ground as more modern supercars, but somehow that doesn't seem to matter. You climb out after a spirited drive feeling as if you've been injected with amphetamine-laced Red Bull. It's just so naughty, so clearly too big for any public road, so god-damn-it-understeery-then-SNAP!-jeeeeeepers-oversteery, it demands full concentration and rewards accordingly.

It is also savagely fast – subjectively every bit as quick as the Aventador that replaced it. The classic V12 may not quite have the rev-range of more modern Lamborghini engines, but its character is more strident and the resulting surges and crescendos of its less-than-perfect calibration make the newer engines seem slightly antiseptic. Not a word you'll ever hear used to describe a Murciélago SV.

SPECIFICATIONS

Years produced: 2002–04 **Engine:** V12, 5,999cc **Max power:** 651bhp @ 7,800rpm
Torque: 485lb ft @ 5,500rpm **0–60mph:** 3.6sec **Max speed:** 217mph
Price: £450,000/$643,300 new in 2002, £1.75m+/$2.25m today

2002

Ferrari *Enzo*

In 2002, Ferrari unveiled a new flagship supercar, named after its founder. It had to be special – and it was

A lmost 20 years on from its launch, the Enzo's shock value remains undiminished, the boldness of its profile, the brutality of its squared-off tail. Still not beautiful in the conventional sense, but magnificent and utterly compelling. So you approach with a certain reverence, as befits a car named in memory of the Old Man himself.

Inside, it's wall-to-wall carbon fibre, no frills or fripperies. Ahead are only the essentials: steering wheel, two pedals, two paddles and big, clear dials. Dab the brake, press the scarlet button and register the shrill spin of the starter motor before 12 combustion chambers ignite in a barrage of furious sound. Dab the brake again, pull back on the right-hand paddle and gently squeeze the throttle. The clutch begins to bite and the Enzo gets moving as the carbon tub transmits all manner of vibrations and resonances into your body. You really do feel like one of the car's components.

Already the 6-litre V12 dominates. Few cars offer such a direct, precise and immediate connection between throttle and response. On slightly damp tarmac, traction control makes clean, uninterrupted progress tricky, so select Race mode to relax the electronic reins. As the Enzo winds through the intermediate gears, revs flaring and tail shimmying as the meat of torque arrives at 4,500rpm, you look for big, open roads on which to unleash its full potential.

The steering is alert and aggressive, enough to require calm hands and measured inputs through fast corners to avoid over-agitating the chassis. Get it settled before you ask it to change direction and it stays deliciously flat and four-square to the road, slicing through like a slot car, punching out onto the next straight.

When you finally get a chance to stoke the V12 through the gears, it's sensational. The sound builds from a deep, rolling bellow to a raw, jagged howl, reaching an aural and accelerative crescendo, each upshift punctuating the aria with a short, phlegmy stammer. The automated single-clutch transmission requires you to finesse the upshifts by easing slightly off the throttle. There's no need on downshifts, so squeeze the brilliantly powerful and feelsome carbon brakes and bang down through the gears, revelling in the *brapp-brapp* blips and crackling report of the exhausts. It might be the early product of a digital age, but the Enzo's thrills are very much of the visceral kind.

2003
Ferrari *360 Challenge Stradale*

Ferrari's line of 'junior' supercars stretched right back to the '60s Dino.

In 2003, they suddenly went hard-core, with the track-inspired Challenge Stradale

SPECIFICATIONS

Years produced: 2003–04 **Engine:** V8, 3,586cc **Max power:** 420bhp @ 8,500rpm
Torque: 275lb ft @ 4,750rpm **0–60mph:** 4.2sec **Max speed:** 186mph
Price: £133,025/$187,124 new in 2003, £150,000+/$210,000+ today

e didn't know it at the time, but the 360 Challenge Stradale would be the first of a whole new breed of Ferraris, now generally known as the 'special series' cars. It was basically a road-going version of the 360 Challenge race car (*stradale* meaning 'road' in Italian), so it was extensively lightened, the suspension retuned and the V8 reworked with titanium components to produce 420bhp at a searing 8,500rpm. The Stradale also shunned the traditional manual gearbox for Ferrari's then market-leading semi-automatic.

Inside, it feels every bit the road-racer, the floors bare metal, the welds on the chassis in full view. Pressing the start button rouses the engine to a harsh, vibratory blare. Hook first with a tug on the massive right-hand paddle, and hit the Race button – the only real driver mode and the one that makes the gearshift speed more acceptable by modern dual-clutch standards.

From the moment the wheels turn, the CS is all about delicacy. There's a button for firming up the damping, but you don't need that on the road, and you can help the gearbox by coming slightly off the throttle for shifts executed at anything less than, say, 80 per cent effort. Flat-shifting when you're really trying works acceptably well; attempting the same in normal driving brings an embarrassing lurch.

There's nothing antiquated about the braking setup, with the carbon-ceramic brakes being donated by the Enzo. It's the braking performance that normally dates an older supercar, but not so here, the CS stopping with convincing enthusiasm and that characteristically abrasive hiss of ceramic discs. Most of all, driving the CS is about what you do as a driver. The whole car feels light, a belief fostered by the effortless but very direct steering, but it's also a car that moves around more on the road than is the modern way – grip levels are lower and there's a much larger window between grip and outright slip, which gives you time to react and adjust the balance.

Unsurprisingly, the V8 engine needs revs to do its best work, and then it feels worth every one of its 400-plus horses, at an exalted rev-range that you would happily drive around in all day. It's a deeply beguiling mix of old and new, the CS, and it set out the template for an entire bloodline.

SPECIFICATIONS

Years produced: 2003–13 **Engine:** V10, 4,961cc **Max power:** 522bhp @ 8,000rpm (Superleggera)
Torque: 376lb ft @ 4,250rpm **0–60mph:** 3.8sec **Max speed:** 196mph
Price: £150,000/$165,000 new in 2003, £90,000+/$58,000 today

2003
Lamborghini *Gallardo*

In 2003, Lamborghini launched its baby supercar, a direct rival for Ferrari's 360 –
especially when it evolved into the hard-core Superleggera

L amborghini's epic V12-engined supercars had long become the stuff of legend. Could a smaller, more agile, more affordable Lambo embody the same Sant' Agata spirit or would something be lost in translation? The Gallardo provided the answer – and it was emphatically positive. The compact new body was unmistakably a Lambo and underneath was an all-new 493bhp 5-litre V10 that loved to rev and a four-wheel-drive system that delivered a new layer of all-road, all-season drivability but still had a distinctly playful side.

The Gallardo went through many evolutions in its ten-year lifespan and one of the first to get fans of hard-core sports cars salivating was 2007's Superleggera. Weight-saving measures pared away a full 100kg/220lb, with carbon fibre now much in evidence, from the shells of the seats to the fixed rear wing, while under the new lightweight engine cover the V10 was now making 522bhp at 8,000rpm.

Twist the key, smile as the starter makes its distinctive helium chuckle, then flinch as ten cylinders pound into life, thundering through a free-breathing exhaust system. Pull back on the right-hand pedal for the slightly clunky e-gear

transmission (a trad manual was also an option) and feel it shuffle clutch and revs as you move away. Every Gallardo feels and sounds tough and mechanical; with minimal sound-deadening, the Superleggera is even more vocal.

It takes all of a mile to appreciate how different it is from a 'full fat' Gallardo. The standard car feels chunky and grippy and weighty; here, you get the muscular feel but with a new sense of urgency and responsiveness. The Pirelli P Zero Corsa tyres generate plenty of grip but also relinquish their hold in a progressive manner. With the ESP switched off, the baby Lambo feels even more alive and responsive to throttle play, a slight lift on turn-in getting the chassis up on tiptoes in a way the standard car can't manage. Get the rear sliding and you can pick it up on the throttle, the 4WD shuffling the torque into a more rear-wheel drive stance. The only black mark is for the optional carbon-ceramic brakes, which have too little bite when you just want to cover the pedal gently, but then grab abruptly when you press harder.

But that doesn't spoil the party. Objectively impressive and subjectively intoxicating, this is a compelling driver's car in the finest Lamborghini tradition.

2004

Porsche *Carrera GT*

Porsche pulled out all the stops for the Carrera GT, its first full-on supercar since the 959

SPECIFICATIONS

Years produced: 2004–07 **Engine:** V10, 5,733cc **Max power:** 604bhp @ 8,000rpm
Torque: 435lb ft @ 5,750rpm **0–60mph:** 3.5sec **Max speed:** 205mph
Price: £323,000/$440,000 new in 20004, £600,000+/$750,000 today

The Carrera GT had motorsport coursing through its arteries. The V10 engine with its dry-sump lubrication system had originally been designed for a Le Mans sports-prototype, while a pure carbon-fibre monocoque kept weight down to a lithe 1,380kg/3,042lb. Suspension followed race-car practice of having inboard springs and dampers actuated by pushrods; the huge brake discs were carbon-ceramic, and each wheel had a single centre-lock nut, again like a racer.

It was a fabulously rapid device – independent testers clocked 0–60mph in 3.5 seconds and 0–100 in 6.8, and this with a conventional six-speed manual gearbox driving just the rear wheels – though it also gained a reputation for its knife-edge handling at the limits of grip. More than a few drivers exploring those limits on a track ended up facing the wrong way when a slide suddenly became a spin. Most, though, simply found it one of the most thrilling and engaging of all ultra-high-performance cars.

Being a Porsche, everything about the CGT is businesslike; the unpretentious interior looks and feels like a 911 or a Cayman. But on the move it's a surprisingly raw car.

The carbon structure transmits road noise and you feel the busy pulse of the V10, which sounds beautiful from the outside but gritty and full of mechanical malice when you're sitting just ahead of it. The steering is super-direct, so you need to give it calm, measured inputs if you're to make the smoothest, swiftest progress, though this can be difficult when ruts and cambers distract it from your chosen trajectory.

The CGT benefits greatly from being on less extreme tyres than the original Michelin Pilot Cups, giving you more feedback, more progression and a bigger window in which to work before grip is finally exceeded. But it's still a car you need to stay on top of. The engine's revs die like a snuffed candle if you're not positive with the pedals and snappy with your gearshifts, and you still need to be ready to make quick corrective steering inputs when traction is breached.

Of course, this makes it a sensationally rewarding car to master, so don't be deceived by the soft curves of its bodywork. They belie a steely, race-bred driving experience built around a wailing V10 of uncommon urgency. Mated to a sharp-shifting manual transmission and a chassis tuned for uncompromising agility, it's a thoroughbred with the finest possible bloodline.

2004

Ford *GT*

Ford's decision to build a modern facsimile of its 1960s multiple Le Mans winner provoked disquiet in some quarters, but it turned out to be an absolute gem

SPECIFICATIONS

Years produced: 2004–06 **Engine:** V8, 5,409cc, supercharged **Max power:** 550bhp @ 6,500rpm
Torque: 500lb ft @ 3,750rpm **0–60mph:** 3.7sec **Max speed:** 205mph
Price: £125,000/$149,995 new in 2004, £250,000+/$335,000+ today

Not everyone jumped for joy when Ford announced it was to build a modern supercar with the looks of its classic 1960s GT40 endurance racer. Some called the new GT a pastiche and lamented what they saw as Ford's lack of imagination. But who needs imagination when you have a back catalogue that can gift you one of the greatest supercar shapes of all time? As soon as the GT appeared in the metal, even the cynics were seduced – especially if it was a Heritage Edition like the car here, in the iconic Gulf racing colours.

Even today, and after the release of the considerably more powerful second-generation GT in 2016, the early Noughties GT has a charisma that draws you in and won't let go. And as a driving machine, it is unequivocally right up there with the very best. Underneath its superplastic-formed aluminium body is a light but stiff aluminium spaceframe chassis, cradling a 5.4-litre 550bhp supercharged V8 (easily tunable to 600bhp and beyond) and a six-speed manual gearbox. The thunderous power is, of course, highly addictive, but within yards it's the overall sense of polish that is truly astonishing.

You fold yourself into the GT, duck and wince as you shut the door, hoping not to be scalped by the section that cuts into the roof. The laid-back driving position is great, and while the GT40-style interior feels a bit cheap, it's wonderfully evocative. The seats are disappointingly unyielding, but that's the last negative your brain registers, whether you go for a gentle pootle on the big waves of torque or rev the V8 to its limiter and push the 345-section rear tyres to the very edge.

'Edge' is actually the wrong word because the GT defies expectations by feeling extraordinarily well-rounded. You expect a heft, a sense of great forces acting on those massive tyres. In fact, everything is light, effortless and shot through with quality. The damping is supple and pours the car across even tricky roads, the shift of the six-speed manual gearbox is sweet and precise, and the steering just perfection: smooth, perfectly weighted and so in tune with the chassis' responses.

It's a car with timeless appeal. And its brilliance lies not just in its nostalgia-tickling styling and glorious V8 engine note but, perhaps most of all, in that beautifully resolved chassis.

SPECIFICATIONS

Years produced: 2005–06 **Engine:** In-line 6-cylinder, 3,996cc **Max power:** 406bhp @ 7,500rpm
Torque: 349lb ft @ 5,000rpm **0–60mph:** 3.7sec **Max speed:** 185mph
Price: £49,995 new in 2005, £75,000+/$97,000+

2005

TVR *Sagaris*

TVRs were always wild, but the Sagaris was the maddest of all. It also happened to be one of the very best – but its life was sadly cut short

While TVR had been around since the 1950s, making glass-fibre-bodied sports cars in Blackpool, Lancashire, the marque rose to prominence in the 1990s with a succession of particularly attractive and charismatic models. Griffith, Chimaera, Cerbera, Tuscan and others won the company legions of fans, and the firm even developed its own engines, which proved suitably powerful and charismatic, if somewhat prone to reliability issues.

The last of this great line was the Sagaris, like its forebears built around a steel spaceframe and in this case with a 4-litre, 406bhp TVR straight-six at its core. Originally conceived as a race-car, it was the most extreme model yet, but also the most thoroughly developed. Road testers loved it. Alas, the company was by now in desperate financial shape and, in 2006, the factory doors closed with just 211 examples built.

Inside is every bit as wild as out, with bespoke aluminium controls and soft leather wrapping the curves and folds. The straight-six sounds a little lumpy at first but gets smoother as it warms through. The brakes squeak a bit and the gearbox requires a deliberate hand, while the assisted steering feels light and a little aloof in the early miles; get some loading into the chassis, however, and it takes on near-perfect weighting, the wheel writhing faithfully in the palms, the chassis working all four corners to confidence-building effect.

The engine doesn't respond with the urgency you might expect, but the unusually long travel of the throttle pedal has something to do with that. It simply accrues speed in a totally linear, inexorable fashion. And then there's the soundtrack. For the full effect you need to drive through a tunnel, or alongside a stone wall, so that the cannon-tube exhausts can fire point-blank at a hard surface. Now crack the window down an inch or two. From 3,000rpm, the TVR's voice is a staccato bark, and as you ease the pedal over its long arc, the bark gets louder and angrier. It builds to a filthy, lumpy snarl at the top end, while bringing the pedal back into the footwell ignites an uneven volley fire of cracks and pops on the overrun.

Cars like this have been badly missed over the last 15 or so years. TVR's return, whenever it comes, is eagerly awaited.

2005

Bugatti *Veyron*

There were supercars and hypercars and then there was Veyron. As a sheer feat of engineering,
the world had never seen anything remotely like the 1,000bhp, 250mph-plus Bugatti

SPECIFICATIONS

Years produced: 2005–15 **Engine:** W16, 7,993cc, quad-turbo **Max power:** 1,000bhp @ 6,000rpm
Torque: 922lb ft @ 2,200–5,500rpm **0–60mph:** 2.5sec **Max speed:** 253mph
Price: £872,000/$1.23m new in 2005, £1.25m+/$1.1m today

Even when you'd digested the stats – 8 litres, 16 cylinders, four turbochargers, 1,000bhp, 253mph, €1.2m plus taxes – nothing could quite prepare you for the first time you unleashed the Veyron's full fury. But somehow the performance wasn't the most remarkable thing about this landmark supercar; it was the way Bugatti's engineers had managed to package all that incredible power and technology into a car that was as temperament-free and as happy to pootle through town as an Audi TT. The Veyron really was that thoroughly developed, that rounded.

The 1,000bhp output was actually a conservative figure; the mammoth W16 engine would regularly see up to 1,100bhp on the dyno. So it's quite a moment if you're ever lucky enough to slip into the exquisitely trimmed carbon-shelled driver's seat and thumb the alloy starter button just behind the gear stick. The engine churns for a couple of seconds then catches with a deep, thunderous growl, overlaid with all sorts of whirrings and whooshings – a vast presence just over your shoulder. Moving off is drama-free; just nudge the gear stick into Drive, release the brake and squeeze the throttle. You can even drive it as a full auto.

The first time you floor the throttle, however, your notion of 'fast' is scrambled forever. The Veyron, big and solid and dense with engineering, transforms into a furious ball of energy. There's tumult behind as four turbochargers blow and 16 cylinders fire. Monstrous torque hits the rear wheels and the car twitches and squirms as its brains and differentials work frantically to contain it. As you're cannoned along the tarmac, your lower legs go momentarily light. Gearchanges come and go so fast and so smoothly you're hardly aware of them. After a few short seconds you're running out of clear road and closing on 150mph. At which point you'll probably burst out laughing.

But it's not all about straight-line speed. It rides well and the steering's beautifully weighted and ideally geared to make the car feel instantly responsive but without a hint of twitchiness. Through fast, sweeping corners the Veyron is simply awe-inspiring. A rock of the shoulders sees the nose turned in, then you can pour in the power and feel all four contact patches sucker onto the road surface as it slices through one corner after another; minimal roll, staggering grip, perfectly poised at 100mph-plus. What a machine.

2006

Audi *R8*

The sheer brilliance of Audi's first mid-engined car took many by surprise, and when it gained a V10 engine, it became a genuine Ferrari/Lamborghini rival

A udi had built some great performance cars over the years, but the R8 was its first mid-engined, two-seater sports car. It first appeared with a 4.2-litre 414bhp V8 and, true to type, was beautifully built and discreetly potent. What wasn't expected was that, despite being fitted with quattro permanent four-wheel drive, when pushed to its limits on a track, the R8 actually handled like a rear-wheel-drive car – and a mightily entertaining one at that.

When the R8 5.2 FSI joined the range in 2009 with a 525bhp version of the Lamborghini Gallardo's 5.2-litre V10 (both cars being part of the same giant Audi-VW group), the performance jumped a whole division, lifting the top speed to 196mph and providing a Germanic alternative to the usual Italian supercar suspects.

Today, an early V8 still feels really special. For some its rev-happy 414bhp V8 and *click-clack* open-gate manual gearshift mean less mass behind and greater balance and agility all round. As soon as its wheels begin to roll, the ride feels supple, the whole drivetrain taut and shot through with quality. It's not eye-wideningly quick, but it's a car whose depth of ability creeps up on you. It doesn't punish indelicate or ill-timed inputs, yet the better you drive it – the gearshift, for example, rewards a finessed approach – the better it feels. Suspension control is exceptional, the R8 gliding over cross-country roads and slicing through corners with the power, control and accuracy of a Federer backhand, all the while engaging and involving the driver with tactility and feedback.

The V10 is an altogether more serious proposition, and never more so than in the 552bhp GT spec, as pictured here, still driving all four wheels but in this case via a six-speed paddleshift automated manual gearbox. That transmission is able to shift with a slurred delicacy into auto mode, applying the V10's massive torque with the deftest touch, yet it can twang neck muscles at full noise.

Unleashed on the Autobahn, the R8 kicks up to a comfortable 130–140mph, feeling magnificently powerful, scything through three-figure bends with utter composure and conviction. And when the back roads are in the grip of winter, then you'll be even more glad of the R8's four-wheel drive, which, in combination with appropriate winter tyres, makes it one of the era's greatest genuinely usable supercars, come rain, sleet or snow. Well, it is an Audi quattro, after all.

SPECIFICATIONS

Years produced: 2006– **Engine:** V10, 5,204cc (R8 GT) **Max power:** 552bhp @ 8,000rpm
Torque: 398lb ft @ 6,500rpm **0–60mph:** 3.6sec **Max speed:** 199mph
Price: £142,500/$110,000 (GT) new in 2006, £60,000+/$55,000+ today

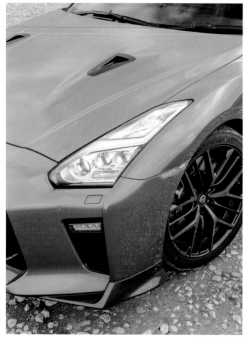

2007

Nissan *GT-R*

The GT-R redefined all-weather all-road performance and brought almost Veyron point-to-point speed within range of ordinary mortals

SPECIFICATIONS

Years produced: 2007– **Engine:** V6, 3,799cc, twin-turbo **Max power:** 562bhp @ 6,800rpm (2017 model)
Torque: 349lb ft @ 5,000rpm **0–60mph:** 2.7sec **Max speed:** 196mph
Price: £79,995/$69,850 new in 2007, £40,000+/$45,000 today

It was the return of Godzilla when Nissan launched the all-new GT-R, successor to the Skyline GT-R series, in 2007. Turbocharging and four-wheel drive were again the main themes, but it was even more densely packed with technology, all the better to outrun any rival on any road and in any weather conditions. Six-speed dual-clutch gearbox, ATTESA E-TS four-wheel drive, VDC-R stability control, electronic launch control, and in place of the Skyline's straight-six, an all-new twin-turbo 3.8-litre V6 producing a very serious 478bhp, enough to rocket it from 0–60mph in 3.2 seconds using that launch control system. The engine's outputs rose even higher as the model received periodic updates, the extraordinary standing-start times dropping even further, until by 2017 road testers were recording 0–60mph in a faintly mind-boggling 2.7 seconds. And this in a car weighing 1,752kg/3,862lb.

It looks like a heavyweight bruiser, too, its chiselled features unremittingly masculine, all jutting jaw and square shoulders. On the move, it's also unremittingly hard-core, with background chatter from all that mechanical hardware and an unforgiving ride. The steering has proper weight to it, but there's feel, too. You can sense the front wheels walking over cambers and pulling at the crown of the road. You feel constantly connected, whether you're doing 10mph or, ahem, rather more. The chatter from the transmission is a permanent backing track but the immense torque and eager self-shifting mode of the gearbox make stop-start driving pretty painless.

Out on fast, open roads, the GT-R's extraordinary performance is laughably accessible. All you need to do is breathe on the throttle and the big-hearted twin-turbocharged V6 fires you down the road with monstrous insistence; you certainly don't need to explore the full rev-range to gain serious speed.

Even on freezing roads, where you'd expect the track-day-style tyres to literally come unstuck, the big Nissan conjures grip like you wouldn't believe, steaming on with apparent disdain for the conditions, engaging you in the process far more than its tech-fest image might have you believe, but not troubling you with many of Isaac Newton's pesky laws in the process. It's a phenomenal car.

So the GT-R won't be to all tastes, but its performance is genuinely jaw-dropping. Very few cars possess such swagger and exuberance, fewer still combined it with everyday practicality, supercar kudos and a sub-£80k/$70k price tag (or as little as £40k/$45k for an early car today). Its legend is well deserved.

SPECIFICATIONS

Years produced: 2007-10 **Engine:** V8, 4,308cc **Max power:** 503bhp @ 8,500rpm
Torque: 347lb ft @ 5,250rpm **0–60mph:** 3.6sec **Max speed:** 198mph
Price: £172,605/$277,455 new in 2007, £140,000+/$232,000 today

2007

Ferrari *430 Scuderia*

Four years on from the 360 Challenge Stradale, Ferrari repeated the recipe with its F430. Even more race-car-like in its performance, the 'Scud' was a sensation

The 'basic' F430 had arrived in 2004, visually an evolution of the 360, although under the skin was an all-new larger-capacity 4.3-litre V8 and a raft of new tech, including an electronically controlled rear differential, or E-Diff, a road-car first. For 2007's Scuderia, just as with the Stradale, the engineers shed weight wherever they could and retuned engine, transmission and chassis for a far more dynamic drive. The result was just scintillating.

It's the Scuderia's powertrain and electronics that move it on comprehensively from the CS. Behind you is a higher-revving, titanium-filled version of the standard 430's V8, and you can tell it's a different engine immediately, with a much harder-edged bark at lower revs. Open the throttle and you're treated to proper accelerative violence and a savage blast of induction roar. This is the Scud's 503bhp making itself felt: an astonishing amount from 4.3 litres of naturally aspirated V8

It feels appreciably faster than the Stradale, and the gearshift helps, too. The single-clutch gearbox had come a long way by 2007, and the shifts are so much faster, at least in the Race setting. That and other modes are accessed by the now-familiar manettino switch on the steering wheel, and with both E-Diff and F1-Trac stability control, the Scud can be seen as a pioneer of the kind of advanced tech we've come to expect in a modern Ferrari. Vitally, these systems are there not just to keep you on the road but to make you look good and let you have fun, all with a safety net in place.

Just as with the CS, there's a lightness of touch to the Scud. There's that same flighty but deft character, just with everything that bit more serious, and not just because of the increased speeds. 'Race' now gathers more of the different systems together but there's also a 'bumpy road' button to slacken the damping off, in which mode this hard-core sports car actually rides well, capturing that all-of-a-piece feel that a well-sorted mid-engined car always seems to exude.

It does still feel raw, though. The V8 dominates proceedings with its strident bark and the hefty torque of a significantly bigger engine kicking the car forward in the mid-range – though of course, being a Ferrari, it still loves to rev. It's a real hooligan, the 430 Scuderia, in a sophisticated, Formula One-inspired suit.

2008

Renault *Sport Mégane R26.R*

Imagine the intensity of a Ferrari Scuderia or Porsche GT3 RS in the form of a hatchback.
That was what Renault Sport delivered with the R26.R

Renault Sport has been responsible for some of the finest driving machines of the last 40 years, but even in that illustrious roll call the R26.R stands out as something very special indeed. Rather as Ferrari did with the Stradale and Scuderia, and Porsche has with its GT3 RS versions of the 911, the engineers at Renault Sport stripped everything out of the already excellent Mégane R26 that wasn't strictly necessary, tautened its sinews, added some sticky track-day-style rubber, squeezed a little more power from the engine and stopping power from the brakes, and set the whole thing off with eye-catching paint and graphics. So if you touch the rear windscreen, you find it's made of polycarbonate rather than glass, and when you drop into the torso-hugging Sabelt racing seat and glance rearwards, you find there's a roll cage where the rear seats used to be.

One of the great joys is that the R26.R rides better than the regular R26, thanks partly to the weight savings delivered by the carbon-fibre bonnet, the plastic rear screen and the absence of trim. And the suppleness of the ride under pressure is key to the ease with which it devours difficult roads. The 227bhp turbocharged 2-litre four seems all the stronger for the lower mass, too, with twin tailpipes blowing gustily and the whistle of the turbocharger adding an extra layer of sonic interest.

With heat into the tyres, carving up a narrow valley road, the Mégane cuts hard and precise into late apexes, inch-perfect between waist-high stone walls, its suspension parrying bumps with the touch of a master. Front-end grip is extraordinary, the chassis displaying an almost unnerving resistance to understeer, which means you can use the transfer of weight to get the tail moving around and play with the balance in minute detail. Agile but calm, absorbent but incisive, it feels effortless at the limit and flattering, too. You find yourself pulling the harnesses down just a little tighter whenever you get a breather on the straights, just because you want to be an ever more integral part of the car, to feel intimately how it's responding.

When it comes to the thrill of driving, the R26.R is one of the most focused cars there has been at any price – and incontrovertible proof that driving thrills are not the preserve of pure sports cars and supercars.

SPECIFICATIONS

Years produced: 2008–09 **Engine:** In-line 4-cylinder, 1,998cc, turbo **Max power:** 227bhp @ 5,500rpm
Torque: 229lb ft @ 3,000rpm **0–60mph:** 5.8sec **Max speed:** 147mph
Price: £23,815 new in 2008, £23,000+/$30,000 today

Aston Martin *V12 Vantage*

When Aston fitted its largest engine into its most compact model,
it created its finest driver's car since the early 1960s' DB4 GT

SPECIFICATIONS

Years produced: 2009–18 **Engine:** V12, 5,935cc **Max power:** 565bhp @ 6,750rpm (S)
Torque: 457lb ft @ 5,750rpm **0–60mph:** 3.9sec **Max speed:** 205mph
Price: £138,000 new in 2009/$179, 995 new in 2011, £70,000+/$80,000 today

A V8-engined version of the Vantage had been around for a few years when Aston hit on the idea of shoehorning its 510bhp 5.9-litre V12 under the bonnet. An outsized engine in a handsome, compact British sports car had obvious appeal, but would the extra weight in the nose wreck the Vantage's inherent balance, and would the rear-wheel-drive chassis be able to handle the extra power without its rear tyres melting?

Any such fears quickly dissipated when road testers got hold of the first examples; the extra power and sonorous soundtrack of the V12 elevated the Vantage onto another plane and the fact that it was wrapped in such a subtly sporting package – only bigger wheels and the cooling vents in the bonnet betrayed the power within – simply made it all the more appealing. Even more performance was to come with the S version, pictured here, the power now up to a Ferrari-worrying 565bhp, lifting the top speed to 205mph – which made it the fastest series-production Aston yet seen.

Settle behind the Alcantara-clad wheel of a V12 Vantage S and one of the first things you notice is that the gearshift is controlled by paddles. They're linked to Aston's Sportshift seven-speed automated manual gearbox, specially beefed-up to handle the S's substantial 457lb ft of torque. There are three-stage adaptive dampers, too. Even in Normal, it's clear the V12V has a tauter setup than any other contemporary Aston, though if you're really pressing on, the extra control of Sport is the mode of choice. The S's extra alacrity through quick direction changes is breathtaking. And with stability control turned off, tight but well-sighted second-gear corners allow you to get on the power early and hold the car in a lovely, long, measured slide.

The V12 engine is simply magnificent, especially in the upper register. And when you need to slow down, the carbon-ceramic discs deliver massive and tireless stopping power without the glassy feel that afflicts some carbon brakes, and in its place a lovely progression and reassurance as the calipers chomp on the massive rotors. The gearbox isn't the swiftest or smoothest, so to finesse upshifts you can lift off the throttle as you pull the right-hand paddle – or simply change gear less and lean on the huge well of torque provided by the engine. And that is no hardship at all.

SPECIFICATIONS

Years produced: 2011– **Engine:** V12, 6,498cc **Max power:** 740bhp @ 8,400rpm (SV)
Torque: 509lb ft @ 5,500rpm **0–60mph:** 2.8sec **Max speed:** 217mph
Price: £321,723/$376,000 (SV) new in 2011, £180,000+/$265,000 (SV £300,000+/$390,000+) today

2011

Lamborghini *Aventador*

Latest in the long line of V12 Lamborghinis, the Aventador delivered all the requisite visual and dynamic drama – especially in wild SV guise

W hile the Aventador inherited the spirit of the Countach, Diablo and Murciélago, it was in fact a completely new car from the wheels up. That included an immensely strong carbon-fibre monocoque and an entirely new 6.5-litre V12 engine, which in the LP700-4 launch model produced 700PS (or 690bhp), enough to propel the new flagship to 217mph. A more sophisticated and capable car than its predecessors, it was, by any objective measure, the best V12-engined Lamborghini ever made. But it didn't quite satisfy those who wanted an edgy, visceral supercar experience from their V12 Lambo. That came four years later, with the LP750-4 Superveloce, or SV for short.

The extreme aero components weren't just for show; the huge rear wing could be adjusted to alter the total downforce and aero balance. The V12 was fiercer than ever, revving to 8,500rpm and producing an extra 50bhp in the process. And to give the chassis more of an edge, the adaptive dampers, four-wheel drive, and speed and load-variable steering were all recalibrated. The combined effect certainly answered any charge of aloofness.

This huge car feels inordinately exciting from the moment you wrench up the door and reverse-fall into the seat. There's carbon fibre everywhere, contributing to a weight saving of 50kg/110lb, but it's the architecture that lends real drama: everywhere you look is alien and outrageous. Now flick up the little red flap to press the engine start button. The braying, gnashing V12, already awe-inspiring in the standard car, is even sharper, even more responsive at low and medium revs, even more terrifying when you find the room and the bravery to wring it out and, of course, even louder.

The seven-speed automated manual was never particularly smooth, and in its faster modes the changes thump home with savage intensity, so the drivetrain has a demonic, sometimes brutal feel. The chassis is where the real changes lie, and here Lamborghini struck a more agile, reactive note. The steering has a more natural, intuitive feel. Nullify initial understeer with a little lift of the throttle, work the accelerator and the SV shows beautiful balance, in the final phase of a corner the rear tyres edging into wheelspin and creating a wicked lick of oversteer.

It doesn't feel as modern and polished as some, largely because of its gearbox, but it's huge fun – at times life-affirming, at times terrifying, but always completely immersive.

2013

Ferrari *458 Speciale*

Next in the line of Ferrari's 'special series' cars was the hard-core version of the 458, which found Maranello at the absolute peak of its powers

SPECIFICATIONS

Years produced: 2013–15 **Engine:** V8, 4,497cc **Max power:** 597bhp @ 9,000rpm
Torque: 398lb ft @ 6,000rpm **0–60mph:** 3.0sec **Max speed:** 202mph
Price: £208,065/$288,000 new in 2013, £240,000/$310,000 today

Not all Ferraris are great. Some are positively mediocre. But the 458 Speciale was – and is – everything you want a Ferrari to be and more. Based on the already brilliant 458 Italia, the pared-back (90kg/198lb lighter), harder-hitting Speciale was a glorious last hurrah for the naturally aspirated 'junior' Ferrari supercar before the turbocharged 488 took over. So at its heart is a stupendous 4.5-litre V8 producing a scintillating 597bhp at a high, high 9,000rpm – enough to launch it from 0–60mph in around 3 seconds and on to the far side of 200mph. And the numbers don't even begin to do justice to the Speciale's appeal.

The first thing you notice is that, in normal driving, it's no more taxing than a 458 Italia, and the ride quality is astonishingly good – especially with the 'bumpy road' mode selected. With nearly 400lb ft of torque and a mass just under 1,400kg/3,086lb, there's instant urge everywhere. But floor the throttle and it absolutely leaps forward; now keep your foot in and get the shift lights on the steering wheel blinking and there's acceleration and a purity of noise that literally takes the breath away. It's this wonderful engine that defines the Speciale, even more than its dazzling electronics,

active aerodynamics and Side Slip Control 2 (yet another advancement in making the driver feel like a hero). In fact, the V8 is just a little bit terrifying when you really wind it all out, while the speed and precision of the shifts from the dual-clutch paddleshift transmission are so downright exciting that they actually add to the whole experience.

From the very first drive, you feel hardwired into the chassis' responses, which means that, despite travelling at extraordinary speeds, you feel oddly calm behind the wheel and able to fully exploit the Speciale's astonishing abilities. Turn-in is breathtakingly aggressive. A nudge of lock and the nose hooks into the corner without a nanosecond's hesitation, the rear ready and eager for throttle. Oblige and you'll feel the rear tyres begin to flare, but progressively, controllably, perfectly.

After 20 minutes, you feel almost drunk on adrenalin and vaguely heroic. There's enough power, sound and drama here to make your skin goosebump like bubble wrap. And every time you climb out of it, ten minutes later you're looking for another excuse to go for a drive. Which says it all, really.

2013
Ferrari *LaFerrari*

Ferrari poured everything it knew into creating a new ultimate road car in the shape of the extraordinary, hybrid-powered LaFerrari

SPECIFICATIONS

Years produced: 2013–17 **Engine:** V12, 6,262cc, plus KERS electric motor **Max power:** 950bhp @ 9,000rpm
Torque: 664+lb ft @ 6,750rpm **0–60mph:** sub-3sec **Max speed:** 217mph
Price: c.£1m/$1.7m new in 2013, c.£3m+/$3.9m+ today

When it comes to pulling out all the stops and building genre-defining flagships, Ferrari never fails to deliver. GTO, F40, F50, Enzo…each was the ultimate in its day, and the LaFerrari built on that heritage with an astonishing fusion of passion and technology, much of it forged in the heat of Formula One battle. That meant a 6.2-litre V12 supplemented by an F1-style KERS (kinetic energy recovery system) electric motor, mated to a seven-speed dual-clutch gearbox and a chassis with adaptive damping, state-of-the-art traction and stability systems, plus the very latest E-Diff 3 electronic rear diff. Perhaps every bit as impressive was the fact that, despite all the extra tech, its dry weight of 1,255kg/2,767lb was exactly the same as its Enzo predecessor.

Compared with the slab-surfaced Enzo, the LaFerrari's body is a complex collision of curves, swoops and active aerodynamic devices. And where the Enzo's cockpit feels hollow and brittle, the LaFerrari's exudes a sense of quality. Start the engine and there's little of the Enzo's bombast, though you're in no doubt of the potency of the powerhouse that sits just behind your shoulders.

Moving off is a cinch, the transmission creamily smooth, the steering weighty with a calm, intuitive rate of response, the damping sweetly controlled, the structure immensely rigid, the refinement high. Which sounds anathema to a Ferrari hypercar but in fact the LaFerrari only filters out the unwanted bits. So the parts that matter – the sense of what each wheel is doing, how much grip is available and how hard the suspension is working – are more clearly gauged and understood. And, thanks to the supremely honed electronics, you have complete faith – and zero frustration – in the driver aids. So while they de-risk the process of cornering quickly, they allow useful slip angles and still put the driver at the heart of things.

The magnitude of performance at the command of your right foot is, frankly, crazy. Work it hard from a standstill and the way the combination of V12 and battery power catapults you down the road is genuinely shocking. Now settle at a steady speed in fifth gear and floor the throttle. Without any hesitation, it thumps you forward, as if you've dropped two gears. In a way, such epic in-gear performance is even more unsettling, and laughably easy. Welcome to the world of the hybrid hypercar.

Porsche *918 Spyder*

Porsche's own hybrid hypercar was a feast of technology with the added attractions of four-wheel drive and truly monstrous torque

SPECIFICATIONS

Years produced: 2013–15 **Engine:** V8, 4,593cc, plus twin electric motors **Max power:** 875bhp @ 8,500rpm
Torque: 944lb ft @ 6,600rpm **0–60mph:** 2.6sec **Max speed:** 214mph
Price: c.£647,000/$845,000 new in 2013, c.£1.5m+/$1.85m today

P orsche has always done things its own way, and the 918 Spyder was very much its own take on the hybrid-powered hypercar: handsome in a traditional way and clearly visually descended from its previous supercar flagship, the Carrera GT. And if it lacked the extreme visual drama of the LaFerrari, the hybrid powertrain beneath its carbon-fibre skin was every bit as impressive. The naturally aspirated race-derived 4.6-litre V8 was supplemented by two electric motors, one for each axle. The net result was that the Spyder hit 62mph/100km/h from standstill in a Veyron-chasing 2.6 seconds but was also capable of a Prius-bashing CO2 figure of 70g/km in official economy tests.

In pure electric mode, the whirring of the electric motors, rustling of the slipstream and insistent squeeze of G-force are new sensory reference points for a new kind of supercar driving experience. Click the rotary control from 'E' for 'e-power' through 'H' for 'hybrid' to 'S' for 'sport hybrid' and the V8 fires in an instant, its hard, ballsy blare erupting from the top-exit exhausts that protrude through the mesh engine cover. The seamless way the 918 segues from electric to hybrid to pure internal combustion and back again is remarkable.

Left to its own devices, its PDK gearbox punches up and down the seven speeds with crisp precision, spookily making up- and downshifts at the exact moment the very same thought crosses your mind. And the way the brakes switch between regenerative braking and the carbon-ceramic discs is little short of miraculous.

Since the engine's power is directed exclusively to the rear wheels, the 918 can be coaxed into a shimmy of oversteer as the rear tyres yield to the assault of truly epic torque (944lb ft of the stuff at its peak). There's rear-wheel steering, too, for added agility. And if you apply the throttle at the right moment, you can feel the motor at the front axle come into play, enhancing traction from corner apex to exit. On a track, you can exit the tighter turns with the throttle pinned, the V8 screaming its heart out, electric motors whirring for all they're worth.

It's a mind-warping demonstration of the 918's prowess and, if a parched mouth and pounding heart are anything to go by, proof that when it comes to delivering an adrenalin rush, the 918 Spyder is up there with the best of them.

McLaren *P1*

The third car in the 'holy trinity' of hybrid-powered hypercars was McLaren's P1,
and in some ways it was the most exciting of them all

SPECIFICATIONS

Years produced: 2013–15 **Engine:** V8, 3,799cc, twin turbo, plus electric motor **Max power:** 903bhp @ 7,500rpm
Torque: 664lb ft @ 4,000rpm **0–60mph:** 2.8sec **Max speed:** 217mph
Price: £866,000/$1.15m new in 2013, c.£2m/$2.6m today

M cLaren set itself a massive challenge with the P1. Not only would it have to stand toe-to-toe with the LaFerrari and 918 Spyder, it would also invite comparison with the immortal F1. No pressure there, then. The P1 certainly had the hardware. With its twin-turbo 3.8-litre V8 and 131kW electric motor both hauling hard, its combined 903bhp trumped the Porsche's 875bhp and came within touching distance of the Ferrari's 950bhp. It had a super-sophisticated chassis, too, with hydro-pneumatic proactive suspension and active roll control, plus a seven-speed dual-clutch gearbox (all the power going to the rear wheels, as in the Ferrari).

In the carbon fibre, the P1 looks dangerously alien with its H. R. Giger-esque curves and hydraulically ramped-up rear wing. As its dihedral door drops shut, its cabin feels intimate, a functional cocoon of exposed carbon with reclined bucket seats. In its more benign settings, it's civilized enough for longer journeys, but dial everything up to one short of Race mode, unleash the horses, and it's totally transformed.

The P1's afterburner-like thrust is overwhelming and addictive. It knows the theatre of speed: the animalistic aggression, the respiratory snorts, chuffs and wheezes of its twin-turbo plumbing, the way its rear wheels seem to be overspeeding, tearing lumps from the road. Driving a fully lit P1 has been likened to riding a firework. And if you deploy the IPAS (Instant Power Assist System), you get the surreal thump of battery power supplementing the V8. It's genuinely like you've pressed the fast-forward button.

The steering strikes an unusual deal between lightness and genuine feel, which is a little disconcerting at first, but it's super-alert and you quickly learn to trust the mighty turn-in grip, then revel in the way the cornering balance can dance to your tune by lifting off or, more satisfyingly, leaning on the vast power reserves.

On track, the full weight of McLaren's F1 know-how and experience coalesce to shattering effect. In Race mode, with suspension lowered and full downforce, the P1 feels insanely fast, super-agile and, unbelievably, supremely friendly. You can adopt quite extreme angles without it biting, and its finely tuned reactions and massive power give endless options. So, P1, LaFerrari and 918 Spyder – different experiences, but all massive fun, and proof that the pursuit of extreme performance needn't be at the expense of simple enjoyment. The new world is like the old world. Only faster.

2014

Koenigsegg *One:1*

Koenigsegg pushed the boundaries of what was possible in a road-going supercar when it launched the One:1, which boasted 1,341bhp and an estimated 273mph top speed

SPECIFICATIONS

Years produced: 2014–15 **Engine:** V8, 5,065cc, twin turbo **Max power:** 1,341bhp @ 7,500rpm
Torque: 1,011lb ft @ 6,000rpm **0–60mph:** 2.9sec **Max speed:** 273mph (estimated)
Price: c.£2m new in 2014, c.£2m/$2.6m today

Swedish supercar maker Christian von Koenigsegg had produced a number of spectacular machines since founding his eponymous company in 1994, but nothing quite like the One:1. Lighter than a McLaren P1, more powerful than a LaFerrari, torquier than a 918 Spyder...he called it 'the world's first megacar' based on its 1 megawatt power output. That equated to 1,360PS, or 1,341bhp in old money, to propel a kerbweight of 1,360kg/2,998lb, hence the One:1.

The headline power figure was produced on E85 bioethanol, but even on normal super unleaded the 5.1-litre twin-turbo V8 was still capable of around 1,300bhp and over 1,000lb ft of torque. Drive went to the rear wheels only, via a seven-speed single-clutch paddleshift gearbox and E-diff. Among Koenigsegg's other claims was a 0–250mph time of just 20 seconds. No wonder road testers approached with a certain trepidation.

The door swings up and out as if filled with helium. You then negotiate a wide sill before tumbling into the thinly padded carbon-shelled bucket seat, the view out through the visor-like windscreen shallow but dramatically panoramic. Press the start button and, after a brief stutter, the V8 wakes up. Not with a big, booming noise, more a hard, flat sound overlaid with busy valve-gear chat. Compared with a 918 or LaFerrari, it's uncouth, but from the moment the hollow-spoked carbon-fibre wheels start to turn, that engine seems to possess the whole car, the noise getting ever harder, deeper and more terrifying.

It's when you flick the right-hand paddle for the third time, feel and hear the gearbox select third, and start to really squeeze on the throttle that previous frames of reference start to fall away in the One:1's wake. By 3,000rpm, the Carrera GT is gone, an Enzo is shrinking away like a diesel supermini. Now 4,500rpm: boom, the P1 and 918 evaporate, the LaFerrari not far behind. From 5,000rpm to the 8,250rpm limiter, all cognitive reasoning gets battered into transmission.

It's no straight-line one-trick pony, though; the damping has a sense of control and a pleasing lightness of touch, and the steering matches it to perfection. It's clearly a car that's been honed to deliver a satisfying dynamic experience, even if it's ultimately not as indulgent as, say, a P1. But the One:1 is very much its own car: devastatingly quick but also agile and truly heart-stoppingly exciting.

SPECIFICATIONS

Years produced: 2014– **Engine:** In-line 3-cylinder, 1,499cc, turbo, plus 96kW electric motor **Max power:** 357bhp @ 5,800rpm
Torque: 420lb ft @ 3,700rpm **0–60mph:** 4.4sec **Max speed:** 155mph (limited)
Price: £99,590/$137,500 new in 2014, £45,000+/$55,000 today

2014

BMW *i8*

Combining a three-cylinder petrol engine with battery power, BMW's i8 provided
a compelling vision of a hybrid future for sports cars

T hat the i8 was fantastic to drive in full electric mode wasn't a surprise – the joy to be had in 23 miles of 129bhp, 184lb ft of torque and a top speed of 75mph with nothing but a soft whirring and the muted gasps of onlookers to disturb the peace wasn't hard to see. Such serene travel remains every plug-in hybrid's party trick, and the conspicuously pretty i8, with its M1-meets-*Minority Report* styling, does it better than most. But the fact that BMW's first hybrid sports car managed to compete with the likes of Porsche's 911 Carrera and Audi's R8 on sheer driver appeal was a genuine surprise.

The 357bhp combined peak power figure when the 1.5-litre three-cylinder petrol engine comes into play certainly helped, but the i8's appeal lay in its bewitching blend of thumping acceleration, superb body control and sheer, wanton desirability.

After you've swung a leg over the high sill of the carbon tub and sunk low into the cockpit, the next thing you notice is the lightness of the carbon door as you pull it shut. Although some of the switchgear would be familiar to an M3 owner, there's a very different feeling to the airy architecture. Push the button, pull back the joystick, squeeze the throttle and the i8 glides off with nothing more than the scrunch of stones beneath its tyres.

Even when the little turbocharged engine kicks in, the refinement of the whole car is so good that it still has an air of calm about it. The steering is very light and lacks any real feel, but it's also clean and precise, and the overall effect is one of ease as you guide the i8 through corners. The supreme ride only enhances the grace of the whole thing. You don't want to push the narrow front tyres too hard, so you're economical with your inputs, carrying speed through corners, occasionally adjusting a line mid-corner with the throttle, making use of the instant torque delivery on the exits. In terms of pace, it's on a par with a contemporary Cayman GTS, and there are moments when you forget the hybrid angle and just enjoy the i8 as a fantastically accomplished 357bhp sports car, the innovative engineering melting into the background.

If hybrid sports cars are the future, on the evidence of the i8, the future's bright.

Lamborghini *Huracán*

The replacement for the Gallardo was hugely impressive – and, in Performante form,
it joined the pantheon of Lamborghini greats

SPECIFICATIONS

Years produced: 2014– **Engine:** V10, 5,204cc **Max power:** 631bhp @ 8,000rpm (Performante)
Torque: 442lb ft @ 6,500rpm **0–60mph:** 2.9sec **Max speed:** 201mph
Price: £215,000/$237,250 new in 2014, £125,000+/$190,000+ (Performante £190,000+/$265,000+) today

The Huracán had so much going for it when it was launched in 2014. Baby Aventador looks, a stunning cockpit with state-of-the-art TFT displays, a mechanical package that included a fabulous 5.2-litre 602bhp V10 engine, seven-speed dual-clutch gearbox, four-wheel drive, carbon brakes and adaptive damping. And, of course, the drama and charisma that come with any Lamborghini. It was rapid and accomplished, too, with a level of finesse never experienced in the outgoing Gallardo, particularly in the gear-changing and braking departments, and massive speed across the ground. But somehow it didn't quite gel as a totally satisfying driver's car or as a truly great Lambo; put simply, it was more about speed and efficiency and less about sheer thrills.

And then, in 2017, came the Performante, pictured here. Supercar watchers had seen plenty of 'special series' cars before but this was different. When it became the fastest standard production car yet timed around the famous old Nürburgring racetrack, people really sat up and took notice.

Its sensational 6:52.01 Nordschleife lap time was down to a number of things, chief among them active aerodynamics, including the dramatic rear wing but also various ducts and flaps that could be manipulated to channel and deflect air to maximum effect. The Performante could even harness the air differently from one side of the car to the other, to make fast cornering even faster. Some 40kg/88lb had been trimmed from the weight, while the high-revving V10 got new intake and exhaust systems, lifting peak power to 631bhp at 8,000rpm. Stiffer suspension, recalibrated steering and stickier tyres completed the package.

The transformation was dazzling – and brought into sharp focus on a racetrack with a regular Huracán. The Performante could accelerate harder, brake later and carry more speed through any given bend. And, oh, the sensations. The taut immediacy as it punched through chicanes; the finger-snap turn-in; the outrageous exit speeds. The rage in the machine just behind your head that, despite the extra power and torque, could be fully exploited in the fastest bends, thanks to the tenacity of the chassis and its active aero reinforcements. And if you just wanted to have fun, the baby Lambo was up for that, too.

In Performante guise, the Huracán was now something very special – the place where seriously fast, focused and exciting meets extraordinarily biddable and forgiving. Its potential had been realized, and how.

SPECIFICATIONS

Years produced: 2015–16 **Engine:** Flat-6-cylinder, 3,800cc **Max power:** 380bhp @ 7,400rpm
Torque: 310lb ft @ 4,750–6,000rpm **0–60mph:** 4.4sec **Max speed:** 183mph
Price: £64,451/$84,600 new in 2015, £70,000+/$98,000 today

2015

Porsche *Cayman GT4*

The mid-engined Cayman had always lived rather in the shadow of the best 911s, but in GT4 form it emerged as an all-time great in its own right

The Cayman and its soft-top Boxster sibling had been around since the late 1990s, and their mid-engined dynamics and refined manners had won legions of admirers through three ever-improving generations. But they'd never quite shaken off the feeling that they were the slightly lesser little brothers to the iconic 911. That all changed with the GT4.

This was the first non-911 to have been developed by the same motorsport engineers responsible for the various iterations of the legendary 911 GT3, and it showed in its performance on both road and track. The basic recipe was a large-capacity naturally aspirated engine (donated by the contemporary 911 Carrera S), a traditional manual gearbox and rear-wheel drive, but the way it had been honed to dynamic perfection was what made the GT4 really stand out.

Approach one today and there's no doubting Porsche nailed the look. The name GT4 seems appropriate for a car whose body components appear to skim the tarmac, whose tyres only just squeeze under the arches and which wears such an enormous wing (adjustable for extra downforce, by the way). Tumble over the side of the hard-edged carbon bucket seat (from the 918 Spyder) and you find yourself sitting bolt upright in front of a perfectly located wheel and pedals.

Should you mind that the Cayman's 380bhp 3.8-litre engine isn't a 'true' Porsche motorsport unit? Of course not. If you'd never driven a GT3, you'd probably think this was the perfect powertrain, with synaptic throttle response, deep-chested mid-range torque that questions the need for turbocharging and a howling crescendo as you reach the 7,600rpm red line. And that six-speed gearbox is one of the finest examples of an H-pattern manual you'll ever experience, with a wonderfully snappy, satisfying action.

The chassis is every bit as impressive as the powertrain, possibly even more so. Nothing seems to have been overlooked in the Cayman's transition from already class-leading sports car to hard-core enthusiasts' machine. It's involving from the moment you move off, with perfect weighting and genuine feel to the steering. Being a Porsche, there are electronic traction and stability systems, which work extremely well, but, being a Porsche, you can also switch them off and revel in the GT4's sublime balance and throttle-adjustability. It's a car that puts driver enjoyment and engagement above the ruthless pursuit of raw performance – and it's all the better for it.

2015

Alfa Romeo *Giulia Quadrifoglio*

A saloon with the passion and performance of a supercar, the Quadrifoglio was
a long-awaited return to greatness for Alfa Romeo

F irst Alfa announced that it was reviving the Giulia name for its new compact saloon. Then it was revealed it would be rear-wheel drive and there would be a 503bhp Quadrifoglio version. Not for the first time, petrolheads dared to dream of a return to form for one of the great Italian marques. Only this time they weren't to be disappointed.

The subtly enhanced Giulia struck the perfect balance of style and sporting intent, with its black mesh bonnet vents, quad exhaust tailpipes and, of course, the cloverleaf enamel badges on the front wings. Inside, you sit behind a virtually upright wheel (thin-rimmed and exquisitely contoured) while adopting a race car-style straight-legged posture, all the better with the optional carbon-fibre-shelled seats. Look ahead and you'll spot the carbon weave in the edge of the bonnet – the material is also used for the boot lid, roof and propshaft.

Philippe Krief, the engineer behind Ferrari's 458 Speciale, had a hand in the Giulia's dynamics, and you soon see and feel his influence. There's the bright red starter button on the steering wheel and the huge metal gearshift paddles linked to the slick eight-speed automatic gearbox. The steering itself is extremely quick, with little more than a quarter of a turn needed for most roundabouts and junctions. The ride is supple, too, just like a Ferrari in its 'bumpy road' setting. Then there's the twin-turbo 2.9-litre V6 (Ferrari-based, although neither side likes to talk about it), which propels the Giulia with a muscular, lag-free delivery.

Switching between driver modes is a piece of panettone. A rotary controller gives you a choice between Advanced Efficiency, Natural, Dynamic and Race, each one ramping up the damper stiffness, throttle sharpness and steering weight.

Even in Natural the Giulia feels alive and connected, the steering delivering just enough useful feedback, while the adaptive dampers soak up bumps while keeping body movements well in check.

Switch to Dynamic and the engine note changes to a deeper timbre, the dampers tense, there's greater heft to the wheel, the stability control takes a step back and the throttle becomes more alert. On to Race and the ESP's shackles are off completely. Yet there's nothing to fear because the transition from grip to slip is progressive, while that wrist-flick steering makes light work of any waywardness.

That's the Quadrifoglio – the saloon with the soul of a supercar.

SPECIFICATIONS

Years produced: 2015– **Engine:** V6, 2,891cc, twin-turbo **Max power:** 503bhp @ 6,500rpm
Torque: 443lb ft @ 2,500–5,500rpm **0–60mph:** 3.9sec **Max speed:** 191mph
Price: £61,300/$75,590 new in 2015, £40,000+/$55,000 today

SPECIFICATIONS

Years produced: 2016– **Engine:** V6, 3,493cc, twin-turbo, plus three electric motors **Max power:** 573bhp (combined)
Torque: 476lb ft @ 2,000rpm **0–60mph:** 2.9sec **Max speed:** 191mph
Price: £143,950/$156,000 new in 2016, £100,000+/$130,000 today

2016

Honda *NSX*

For its second NSX, Honda went down the hybrid route, packing its new supercar with
Porsche 918 Spyder levels of tech at a fraction of the price

T he NSX is just the sort of supercar that an engineering-led company like Honda should build. Twin-turbo 3.5-litre V6 with 500bhp and 406lb ft of torque, bolstered by a trio of electric motors: one between the engine and the nine-speed (count 'em) twin-clutch gearbox, delivering its 47bhp to the rear axle, plus a pair of 36bhp motors acting on the front wheels. The contribution of these motors is made at different phases of the rev-range, so the maximum you get at any one time is 573bhp and 476lb ft. That's still serious heft, the upshot being that the NSX leaps from 0–60mph in under 3 seconds.

Despite the incredible levels of tech, it's actually very intuitive to simply jump in and drive. The cockpit is busy but well laid out, the driving position spot-on. As you'd expect, there are a multitude of driving modes, accessed via a rotary control. In the Quiet setting, you can waft along in pure electric mode. Nudge to Sport and there's tangible energy and intent, the dampers increasing in tautness but striking a nice balance between suppleness and support.

If you didn't know it was a hybrid, you'd think it had an absolute mutha of an engine tucked behind your shoulders. If you concentrate, you'll detect a faint depletion of shove once the electric motors have done their bit up to 4,000rpm, but, in truth, the sensation of slingshotting out of corners and down the road is all-consuming.

Upping the ante to Sport+ is where you really feel the NSX is turning up the heat, with more weight in the steering, more immediacy in the power delivery and greater firmness in the damping. The nine-speed dual-clutch transmission is one of the best, with ultra-clean and eerily prescient up- and downshifts when left to its own devices, though it's more fun to flip the paddles yourself. The steering is alert, the front end blessed with terrific bite, almost too much in tight corners where the tail can be unsettled, though stability control brings it back into line. Through faster turns the NSX is calmer but still incredibly agile. Let loose on moorland roads, it's spellbinding. Not exuberant like a Ferrari, but connected, effortlessly quick and admirably light on its feet without divorcing you from the excitement of driving. It could have been a cold and calculating science experiment, but this is a Honda with real soul.

2016
Bugatti *Chiron*

No other car combined so much luxury with such unimaginable potency as the 1,479bhp Chiron, successor to the mighty Veyron and the first road car to top 300mph

SPECIFICATIONS

Years produced: 2016– **Engine:** W16, 7,993cc, quad-turbo **Max power:** 1,479bhp @ 6,700rpm
Torque: 1,180lb ft @ 2,000–6,000rpm **0–60mph:** 2.4sec **Max speed:** 261mph (limited)
Price: c.£2.5m/$2,998,000 new in 2016, £2.5m+/$3.25m today

Chiron was born to be the new benchmark by which all other hypercars would be judged. And, as with its predecessor, the numbers remain impossible to ignore: £2.1m/$2.5m before taxes; 16 cylinders; four turbos; 1,479bhp; 1,180lb ft; 0–124mph in 6.5 seconds; restricted top speed of 261mph; unrestricted top speed of 280mph (and a world record 304.77mph in pre-production Super Sport 300+ form). Even in a world inured to outrageous figures, the stats are mind-blowing. Inside and out, it's clearly not a car derived from motorsport DNA, but that somehow creates a bigger wow factor in a sector dominated by quasi road-racers. The docked tail and extensive use of mesh is explicit evidence of the furnace-like heat that needs to be extracted from the engine bay, yet the monolithic arc of machined alloy that forms the full-width tail-light is pure art. Such are the glorious contradictions from which this car is composed.

The Chiron doesn't conform to regular hypercar rules. Its motor pulses and rumbles rather than yelps and howls. It's genuinely comfortable to sit in. The fit and finish are fabulous. And, if you can get beyond the heart-thumping realization that you're in a Chiron, it's absurdly easy to drive at ordinary speeds.

Is there a sense of connection? Yes, albeit one that's finely filtered, clear and uncorrupted. You do have an accurate sense of what each corner of the car is doing. You can feel the Chiron working beneath you as you power it through a corner or brake hard after devouring a straight. There's a sense of life and energy – immense forces being tamed and channelled into the tarmac. And there's enough warmth and tactility to make a bond with the machine.

And what of that straight-line performance? Winding the Chiron up to 236mph – the first of its two-stage speed limiters – takes no more effort than hitting the 155mph limiter in a BMW M4. If anything, it feels more impressive the faster you go, with sixth and seventh gears feeding that relentless, runaway feeling of a big airliner in the final few seconds before takeoff.

It's this combination of remarkable efficiency and remorseless violence that's most shocking, and Bugatti at its best. It's an altogether different kind of performance, one that seems genuinely inexhaustible and makes a P1 or LaFerrari feel flaccid. The Chiron hefts you towards the horizon in an unbroken rush while the others huff and puff through the gears. Utterly extraordinary.

2017

Honda *Civic Type R*

It smashed the front-wheel-drive lap record around the Nürburgring, but there's so much more to this bewinged Honda

SPECIFICATIONS

Years produced: 2017– **Engine:** In-line 4-cylinder, 1,996cc, turbo **Max power:** 316bhp @ 6,500rpm
Torque: 295lb ft @ 2,500–4,500rpm **0–60mph:** 5.7sec **Max speed:** 169mph
Price: £30,995/$34,700 new in 2017, £25,000+/$34,000+ today

When the latest Civic Type R burst onto the scene in 2017 with its massive rear spoiler, it was like a throwback to the days when Imprezas and Evos ruled the practical performance car world. Youngsters loved its wild looks, though it was a safe bet that some grown-ups steered clear for the same reason. But that was their loss, because in doing so they denied themselves one of the great fast hatch experiences. This Honda is astonishingly good, not simply in what it does but how it feels and, ergo, how it makes you feel.

And it does it right from the off. The seats are superb and low slung, the gearshift snappy, the pedal spacing ideal, the throttle response of the turbo engine pleasingly sharp. In fact, it drives like all the spoilers and scoops say it will: its steering is direct, slack-free and beefy; its chassis has a tautness that suggests a bias for smooth, warm asphalt; and its brakes bite right from the top of the pedal. Not that everyday comfort and usability were sacrificed for that 7-minute 43.8-second Nürburgring time. Across craggy country roads, the Civic treads so deftly, so calmly, that you can't help but smile.

The last car that had this ability was the Renault Mégane R26.R, and it did so for the same reasons, dishing up wonderfully engaging handling *and* a superb ride. Like the R26.R, the Civic makes every corner an opportunity to experience a little magic. Commit it hard to a turn and you'll feel it slice immediately for the apex – no response lag, no tyre slip – and if you then give it full throttle, it will simply accelerate. No wheelspin, no widening of the line and absolutely no corruption through the steering wheel. The engine's a gem, too, managing to sound and feel like a gutsy naturally aspirated in-line four with a thrilling top end.

For £30K/$35k (or less secondhand) you get a car that will reach 170mph, stay with just about anything on the road, look after the novice driver but involve the experienced, feel completely at home on a track day without so much as a tweak of anything, and be entirely usable everyday. It has some fine rivals – the Focus RS and Golf R chief among them – but by some margin the mad-looking Civic is the daddy. So good, in fact, that you'd be mad to ignore it.

2017

Alpine *A110*

Enthusiasts have delighted at the return of the Alpine name, all the more so because the petite new A110 is far more than just a pretty face

The first thing that strikes you when you approach the A110 is how small and low it is. What really makes it special, though, is how *light* it is. The French manufacturer decided from the outset to invest in aluminium construction, and an impressive 94 per cent of the body and chassis is made of the stuff. The result is that the mid-engined, rear-wheel-drive A110 tips the scales at just 1,103kg/2,432lb, substantially less than rivals, and that makes a big difference on the road.

Hidden beneath the wrap-around rear screen is the all-new, all-aluminium turbocharged 1.8-litre in-line four-cylinder engine, mounted in a bespoke aluminium sub-frame and coupled to an evolution of the Renault Clio's dual-clutch gearbox. Thumb the big orange button on the centre console and the noise it makes when it fires up is clean and sweet. There's a lightness to the way it responds when you blip the throttle, too, and a hollow bark when pulling hard, overlaid with turbo-spooling whoosh. More important, it feels properly sparky – well up to the task, though that's as much to do with the mass of the car. Squeeze on the throttle and, after a moment's hesitation, the Alpine surges down the road, a quick and seamless upshift providing unbroken acceleration.

Then there's the way the Alpine feels on the road, how it reacts to steering inputs and bumps and bends. It feels genuinely light, through the electrically assisted steering and its connection to the road, as if the front tyres are even slimmer than their 205/40 R18 dimensions. The ride feels loose-limbed and long-legged, helping create a unique impression of suppleness. On moorland roads, the car flows along with a lightness of touch that's almost magical, smoothing the surface, composed, effortlessly responsive to your inputs.

It's impressive on a track, too. Even when the Alpine kicks its tail out, you can use it to steer the car with surprising precision, partly because the tail doesn't keep on going – and, again, that's thanks to low mass and inertia. The reimagined A110 feels like a breath of fresh air: modern and classic French all at the same time.

SPECIFICATIONS

Years produced: 2017– **Engine:** In-line 4-cylinder, 1,798cc, turbo **Max power:** 249bhp @ 6,000rpm
Torque: 236lb ft @ 2,000–5,000rpm **0–60mph:** 4.5sec **Max speed:** 155mph (limited)
Price: £51,805 new in 2017, £50,000+/$65,000+ today

2018

McLaren *Senna*

Designed for the track but mind-blowing on the road, the Senna was built to provide maximum driving thrills. And that's exactly what it delivers

SPECIFICATIONS

Years produced: 2018– **Engine:** V8, 3,999cc, twin-turbo **Max power:** 789bhp @ 7,250rpm
Torque: 590lb ft @ 5,500–6,700rpm **0–62mph:** 2.8sec **Max speed:** 211mph
Price: £750,000/$837,000 new in 2018, £1m+ today

Right from the start, the Senna was to be a no-compromise machine. McLaren certainly wasn't bothered about creating a pretty car. The Senna is a preposterous-looking device, but to spend any time with it is to quickly fall in love with its alien form and the sheer joy of something this bonkers wearing number plates. The key stats: 789bhp, 1,198kg dry, 0–62mph in 2.8 seconds, 669bhp per ton and 800kg of downforce at 'only' 155mph.

Slip into the carbon-shelled seat. Even by McLaren's formidable standards the driving position is exceptional, with a sightline straight down to the road's surface. You can drive it slowly, thanks to its fanatically honed twin-clutch gearbox. And it rides well, even when you switch from Comfort to Sport modes for the chassis and powertrain. Yes, its hydraulically interlinked damping has an inherently stiff-legged approach below 20mph, but the faster you go, the better it gets. Meanwhile, the steering chatters, cajoles ands informs in a constant conversation of astonishing clarity.

The Pirelli Trofeo Rs are so sticky to the touch it's like squeezing liquorice between your fingers, and cornering grip is further enhanced by the invisible hand of downforce.

The sense that it's squeezing the Senna into the tarmac is palpable, the stability it imparts hugely confidence-inspiring.

No other hypercar is quite so raw. There's no radio, or carpets, and no air-con. So you notice the heat soak when stationary, but the tiny side windows that drop below the split-line supply fresh air without any buffeting at speed. The M840TR engine, like all McLaren V8s, is a tool for the job and not about enriching the soul. The noise it makes is brutal.

It feels heavily torque-restricted in the first two gears, but switch the ESP to Dynamic, or off, and it's like being strapped to the nose cone of a ballistic missile. Even on a dry road, the fat, sticky Pirellis spin up at the top of first and second gears, the tail swaying from side to side in the pursuit of traction.

Into third, the speed readout is a blur and a corner is approaching. But you know you can brake impossibly late; you know the giant ceramic discs and parachute-like rear wing rotating forwards will haul the Senna down, and more convincingly than in any car you've driven before. It's the final element of an experience that's utterly absorbing, enriching, unforgettable.

Porsche *911 GT3 RS*

There have been GT3 versions of every 911 for two decades, and they've all been brilliant.

Representing them here, the 991.2 generation RS

SPECIFICATIONS

Years produced: 2018– (991.2) **Engine:** Flat-six, 3,996cc **Max power:** 513bhp @ 8,250rpm
Torque: 347lb ft @ 6,000rpm **0–60mph:** 3.2sec **Max speed:** 193mph
Price: £141,346/$187,500 new in 2018, £200,000+ today

I t's always good to get back into a GT3 RS. A 911 might not have the seductive swagger of an Italian supercar, but RSs have long been blessed with a different kind of allure. One that crackles with intent.

The latest version of the 4-litre flat-six engine has 200rpm more to offer, taking the red line to 9,000rpm, the output peaking at 513bhp. At chassis level, there are stiffer springs and race-style rose joints (also known as heim joints) for increased feel and precision, while revised aero give more downforce but less drag.

The 911 has changed much over the decades, but the simplicity of the cockpit is the same, the lack of fuss focusing you on the driving. From the moment you start the engine, there's a feeling of getting down to business. There's plenty of road noise and the ride is hard, but there's enough pliancy to suggest the springs and dampers simply crave loading to settle into their operating window. And you soon relax into the driving, largely because you feel so completely connected to each corner of the car. It's the blend of steering weight, front-end response and the clean yet highly detailed feel you get through your hands. As you push harder, you realize that even among the constellation of fabulous RSs, this latest one shines with rare brilliance. Its extra stability means you can carry significantly more speed deep into the heart of a corner, then lean on the exceptional traction to fire you out.

The engine is utterly sensational – even though you rarely get the opportunity to fully extend it on the road. No matter, for it sounds fabulous through the mid-range: deep and packed with character as it begins to get on top of the low and intermediate gears, before ceding to a steely shriek as you chase that magical 9k red line.

The PDK gearbox is uncannily good, with shifts that snap home rapidly but also effortlessly at modest speeds, yet crack home with synaptic immediacy when you're absolutely on it. In fact, it's so good that not once do you crave the need to slot home each gear with a lever. Besides, it's not like there's a shortage of things to connect your senses to this fabulous machine. The boss of Porsche's GT cars, Andreas Preuninger, describes it as, '11,000 parts working as one', which just about hits the nail on the head.

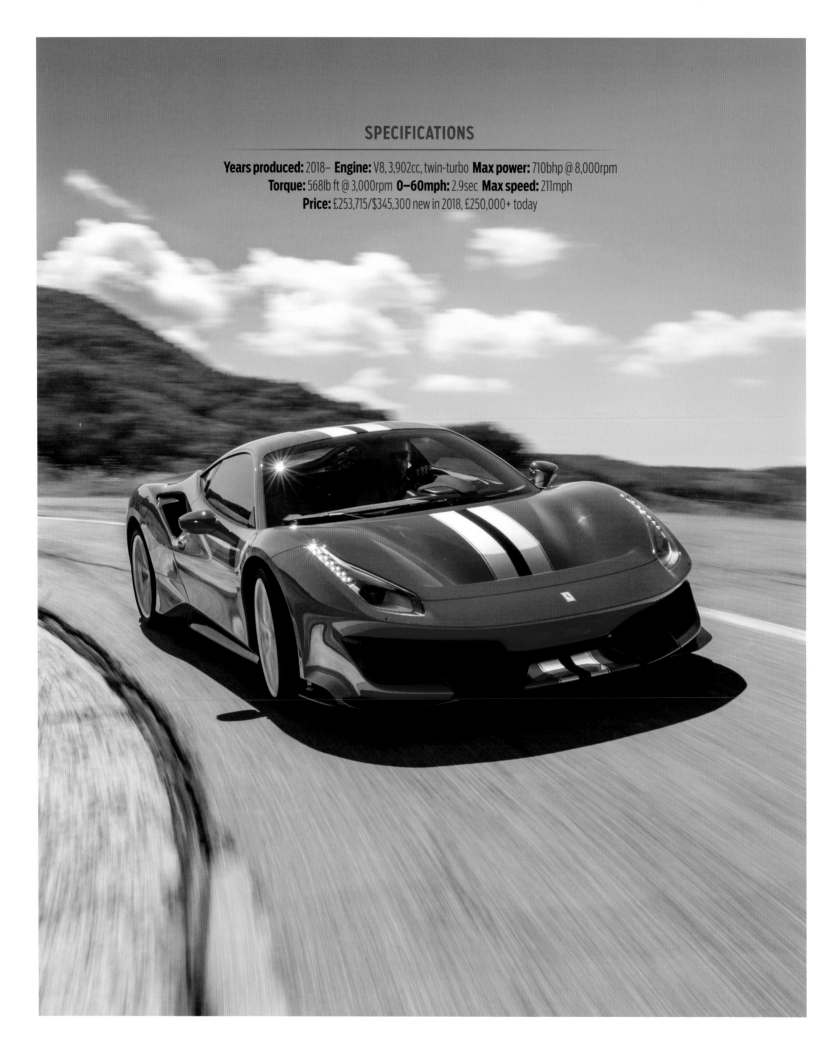

SPECIFICATIONS

Years produced: 2018– **Engine:** V8, 3,902cc, twin-turbo **Max power:** 710bhp @ 8,000rpm
Torque: 568lb ft @ 3,000rpm **0–60mph:** 2.9sec **Max speed:** 211mph
Price: £253,715/$345,300 new in 2018, £250,000+ today

2018

Ferrari *488 Pista*

Latest in the special series of hard-core Ferraris, the Pista poses the question: can you actually have too much performance for the road?

hallenge Stradale. Scuderia. Speciale. Pista. For once, the translation doesn't fall in the Italians' favour with the 488 'Track', but the intent is obvious. Just as with its forebears, the Pista is, in effect, a road-going version of Ferrari's current Challenge one-make racer, without the rear wing, racing wheels and rubber, and motorsport safety equipment. In this case, it means a track-honed, hard-core version of the already-mighty twin-turbo 488 GTB, and the transformation is the most far-reaching yet.

The engine is lightened and reworked to produce an astonishing 710bhp, the overall weight reduced to 1,385kg/3,053lb (or 1,280kg/2,822lb without fluids). The bespoke aero package includes an F1-inspired 'S-duct' in the

nose to force the passage of air through a narrow opening before spitting it out over the steeply rising bodywork. The electronics are the most sophisticated yet.

So you close the door with a tug of a fabric pull and awaken the V8 with a prod of the bright red button on the steering wheel. *Whumph, BURRRRRRR.* It's a deep, granite-edged tenor that reverberates around the interior. On the move, the hollow-timbre bark rises sharply with the merest suggestion of provocation, overlaid by a reserved but sinister hiss from the turbos.

The initial snap forward is just the opening jab; the haymaker follows as the revs rise, because the engine just doesn't give up, power and torque building in formidable

fashion. The power curve actually peaks at 6,750rpm, but then holds constant to 8,000rpm. The effect is almost overwhelming, and using the top third of the rev-range is genuinely a challenge, a test of courage – not only due to how quickly you'll be travelling, but also how endangered your licence will be.

Now you explore the chassis modes. Sport is the 'normal' setting, Race the one that gives you the full-fat mechanical experience, but CT Off is where things get really interesting. In this mode, there's still support from the ESC system (removing that is one more twist and hold of the dial) but it's where Ferrari's new trick acronym really gets to work – the dubiously named Ferrari Dynamic Enhancer. It's essentially a way of making the Pista driver look a lot better than they are. It will let you power-oversteer the car for yards on end, while all the time loitering in the background, ready to step in if the situation does get out of control.

The way in which you can take apart a good road in the Pista is sensational. Turn-in is electrifying, the steering light but not overly so, its precision unerring. But only on track can you let it have its head and not worry about the consequences. Here, there's a dizzying sense of exhilaration about watching the shift lights illuminate on the steering wheel, the ludicrous speed of the gearchange, and feeling the carbon-ceramic brakes bite so resiliently time after time. Here, too, all the electronics systems combine to flatter the driver. The Pista manages to combine a surprisingly friendly demeanour, almost avuncular, while also being so manically fast and powerful that you step unsteadily from the car with eyes wide and breathing short.

Allowed to run wild, the Pista is beyond astonishing, but that's on a circuit, not on the road, where it's a prisoner much of the time. That's not Ferrari's fault per se: the market demands every new car is faster and more powerful than the last, and this is where we've ended up. Where we go from here is unsure, but in the meantime, in pure objective terms, there's probably never been a better Ferrari than the amazing 488 Pista.

McLaren *600LT*

Below its P1 and Senna hypercars, McLaren has produced an almost bewildering range of cars in recent times. For sheer fun, none matches the 600LT

SPECIFICATIONS

Years produced: 2018– **Engine:** V8, 3,799cc, twin-turbo **Max power:** 592bhp @ 7,500rpm
Torque: 457lb ft @ 5,500–6,500rpm **0–60mph:** 2.9sec **Max speed:** 204mph
Price: £185,500/$256,500 new in 2018, £200,000+ today

In the McLaren model hierarchy, the Sports Series means the most affordable models, a line that started with the 12C back in 2011 and currently stretches to the car you see here. 'Longtail', meanwhile, a name first associated with the 1990s F1 GTR racer, represents a sort of hard-core sub-brand, rather like Porsche's RS range. The 600LT, then, is the first hard-core Sports Series. If you think of it as something like a 911 GT2 or GT3 RS, you're not too wide of the mark.

The important thing is that, just like the Senna but at a rather more accessible price point, the 600LT was created for people who really care about driving. It isn't about raw power, although it does boast 592bhp from its 3.8-litre twin-turbo V8, up from 562bhp in the 570S on which it's based. More noteworthy is the 84kg/185lb reduction in weight (88kg/194lb if you spec the optional carbon front wings and roof) to 1,356kg/2,989lb. The Longtail moniker is justified by a 47mm-/almost 2in extension to the car's rear, complemented by a 27mm-/1in-longer splitter at the front. The increased manipulation of air means there's now 100kg/220lb of downforce at 155mph, compared to the neutral figure of the regular car, but with no penalty in drag. Under the carbon-fibre skin are new forged alloy wishbones, stiffer and hollow anti-roll bars, recalibrated dampers and huge carbon-ceramic disc brakes.

The transformation is remarkable. Where the 570 when hard-pressed introduces just a hint of vagueness, of squidge and imprecision, everything the 600LT does is ruthlessly, but delightfully, transparent and true. It feels raw and nuggety, engine vibrations throbbing through the cabin. As you hit open countryside, gone is the 570's light touch and almost magical indifference to ravaged tarmac, replaced with positively fibrous feedback, laser-like resolve and ride quality that connects, unfiltered, with the road.

There is immense speed on offer here (62mph takes 2.9 seconds; 0–124mph just 8.2) though in a way the braking performance is every bit as impressive. Stopping power is formidable, the car's stability under braking exemplary, and the pedal has a perfect weighting that's reproduced in all the major controls. Most of all, when it finally relinquishes grip, adjustability on the throttle mid-corner is as deft as you can manipulate with your right foot. It is, quite simply, one of the best-handling cars ever created. Oh, yes, and it spits blue flames from its high-mounted exhausts. What's not to like?

2019

Renault *Mégane RS Trophy R*

The Trophy R is more extreme – and more expensive – than any hot hatch yet seen.

And we may never see anything quite like it again

A fter 40-odd years of hot hatch history, the relentless march of technology, evolving social attitudes and market trends, a car arrived in the summer of 2019 that blew the hot hatch ceiling into tiny fragments. In the ripe, mellow, autumnal days of the pre-electrification internal combustion engine's lifetime, the exotic and eye-wateringly expensive Trophy R is as focused, uncompromising and ears-pinned-back-fast as a hot hatch has ever been – and might ever be.

Just 500 are to be built, with prices starting at a faintly absurd £51,140 but rising to a truly jaw-dropping £72,140 with the 'Nürburgring Pack' of ultra-lightweight components, including carbon-fibre wheels and immense carbon-ceramic brake discs, in which form the Trophy-R set a new hot hatch 'Ring lap record of 7min 41sec.

Visually, it nods to its papa, the Mégane 265 Trophy, and of course its grandpapa, the inimitable R26R of 2008, looking suitably menacing with its bare carbon bonnet duct. Open the door and the interior is unremittingly dark and simple. The voracious 296bhp turbo four-pot shatters the silence, echoing through the interior void and thrumming gently through the seat. In full-bore acceleration mode, its raw aggression is everything that's great about turbocharged engines in lighter cars. There's something captivating about an angry turbo motor greedily consuming boost and responding urgently – that sudden flare of revs, snapping you and the car forwards and spiking your adrenaline.

On a twisty backroad, it feels as excitable as a five-year-old with a secret stash of Haribo, bucking, weaving, hopping, snarling, popping and banging, a car straining to go flat-out and, at the same time, yearning to hit its stride. Whether travelling that quickly on a public road to access that enjoyment is healthy or not is another matter.

On the road, the very firm damping can actually be a hindrance, but on track the Trophy R is instantly at home. The brakes can be tricky to modulate, but their ultimate power and endurance is superb. That's something that applies to the whole car, for the R shrugs off hard track work like few other mainstream cars, refusing to wilt even when pushed really hard. Grab it by the scruff and it's a ball of nuclear energy.

SPECIFICATIONS

Years produced: 2019– **Engine:** In-line 4-cyl, 1798cc, turbo **Max power:** 296bhp @ 6000rpm
Torque: 295lb ft @ 3200rpm **0-60mph:** 5.3sec **Max speed:** 163mph
Price: £51,140+ new in 2019, £50,000+/$64,000+ today

Aston Martin *Valkyrie*

Designed by F1 genius Adrian Newey, the Valkyrie is set to redefine every performance parameter

for a roadgoing hypercar

SPECIFICATIONS

Years produced: 2020– **Engine:** V12, 6.5 litres, plus battery-hybrid system **Max power:** 1000bhp @ 10,500rpm (plus 130bhp)
Torque: 546lb ft @ 7000rpm **0–62mph:** c2.5sec **Max speed:** c250mph
Price: c.£3m/$3.2m (est) new in 2020

The Valkyrie is Adrian Newey's vision of the ultimate supercar, much as the McLaren F1 was for fellow genius race-car designer Gordon Murray, and it's been co-developed by Aston Martin and Red Bull Advanced Technologies. As with the McLaren, absolutely no compromises have been made in pursuit of the purest, most intense driving thrills.

So the Valkyrie's sensational, Cosworth-built V12 engine produces 1,000bhp – and that's without any sort of turbocharging or supercharging. There has never been a naturally aspirated road car engine like it. Now add another 130bhp from a battery-hybrid system and consider that the Valkyrie weighs just 1,100kg/2,425lbs, and throw in the fact that its aerodynamics will deliver race-car levels of downforce, and all in a package much smaller and more agile than any other hypercar yet seen. No wonder car enthusiasts are on tenterhooks to find out just how sensational it will be behind the wheel.

The first running prototype broke cover in the summer of 2019, but by then test drivers had already clocked up tens of thousands of miles in the virtual realm, using state-of-the-art simulators, in exactly the same way that today's F1 cars are designed and engineered. And a handful of journalists were invited to Red Bull HQ to drive the virtual Valkyrie for themselves and get a taste of what's in store.

The reclined, feet-up driving position of the sim is actually pretty close to the Valkyrie's as we set off on a virtual lap of the famous Spa-Francorchamps circuit, initially driving a 'benchmark car' that combines the best bits of various Ferrari, McLaren and Porsche supercars. Swapping to the Valkyrie is a surreal step. It accelerates much more intensely, Spa's pixilated scenery fizzing by much, much more quickly. The leap in performance is remarkable, especially in the high-speed corners.

What's just as impressive is how controllable the Valkyrie feels even when you take huge liberties with it. Its limits are sky-high, but once you reach them not only are they tangible, but you can lean on them, exceed them and come back from them without feeling that you're juggling chainsaws. Appetite well and truly whetted.

The next chapter in the story of the supercar is being written, and if we're reaching the end of the road for the pure, naturally aspirated, internal combustion engine, then what a glorious way to sign off!

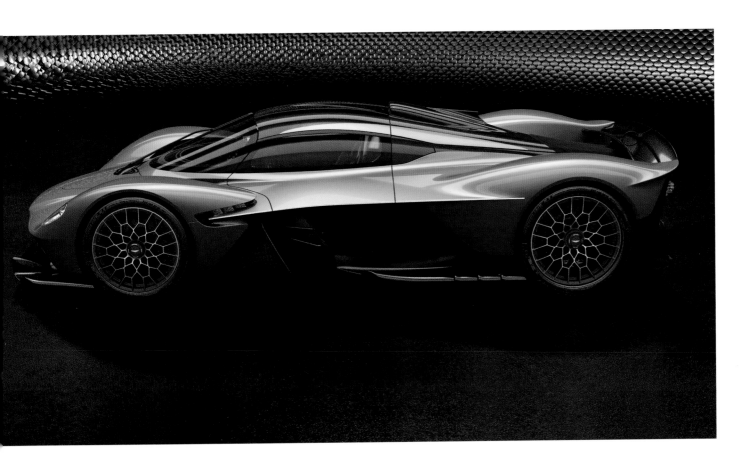

Index

An Hachette UK Company
www.hachette.co.uk

First published in Great Britain in 2020
by Mitchell Beazley,
a division of Octopus Publishing Group Ltd
Carmelite House, 50 Victoria Embankment,
London EC4Y 0DZ
www.octopusbooks.co.uk
www.octopusbooksusa.com

Copyright © Octopus Publishing Group 2020
Text Copyright © Dennis Publishing Limited 2020
EVO and Octane are registered trademarks of
EVO Publications Limited and Dennis IP Ltd respectively.

Distributed in the US by Hachette Book Group
1290 Avenue of the Americas, 4th and 5th Floors,
New York, NY 10020

Distributed in Canada by Canadian Manda Group
664 Annette St., Toronto, Ontario, Canada M6S 2C8

ISBN 978 1 78472 595 2

A CIP catalogue record for this book is available from
the British Library

Printed and bound in China

10 9 8 7 6 5 4 3 2 1

Commissioning Editor: Joe Cottington
Design: Jeremy Tilston
Senior Editor: Alex Stetter
Production Controller: Allison Gonsalves
Consultant on US prices: Marc Noordeloos
Text compiled by Peter Tomalin

Photographer Acknowledgments

Tim Andrew 74-75; Aston Martin 176-177, 218-221;
Michael Bailie 72-73; Mark Dixon 14-15, 18-19, 24-25,
40-41, 57; Max Earey 140-141; Drew Gibson 147; Martyn
Goddard 29, 32; Gus Gregory 4-5, 36-37, 101, 158-159, 161;
Malcolm Griffiths 148-149, 150; Stephen Hall 98-99, 170;
Paul Harmer 16-17, 30-31, 34-35, 42-45, 48-49, 52-53, 58-
59, 60-61, 77, 86-86, 138-139; Honda 137; Matt Howell 6-7,
50-51, 66-69, 71, 84-85, 142-143, 153; James Lipman 8-9,
38-39, 80, 123; Ian McLaren 20, 26; Lyndon McNeil 46-47;
Charlie Magee 10-11, 62; Andy Morgan 82-83, 105, 114-115;
Kenny P 167; Aston Parrott 64-65, 92-93, 97, 118-119,
124-125, 127, 128-131, 132-133, 134, 156-157, 172-173, 174-175,
178-179, 181, 193, 194-195, 197, 200-201, 203, 204-205,
206-207, 209, 210-213, 214, 217; Chris Rutter 90-91; Tom
Salt 78-79, 88-89, 94-95, 108-109; Tim Scott 12-13; Dave
Smith 168-169; Dean Smith 2-3, 54-55, 110-113, 120-121,
144-145, 154-155, 162-163, 164-165, 182-183, 184, 187,
188-189, 190-191, 198-199; Alex Tapley 106; Henri Thibault
22-23; Matt Vosper 116-117